THE ADVENTURES OF

UNCLE BILLY

AND

ROSS

Life Lessons Made SiMpLe

Solon Phillips, ESQ

A'Lure Publishing, LLC

Copyright © 2024, 2021 by Solon Phillips, ESQ

Printed in the United States of America
Library of Congress Control Number: 2024905312
ISBN: Paperback   979-8-9902920-0-0

Republished by   : A'Lure Publishing, LLC
Publication Date : April 26,2024

For Information Contact
alurepublishingllc@gmail.com
www.alurepublishing.net T: 919-391-8502

Book Cover Designed by K.L.M. DESIGZ & Printz

ACKNOWLEDGEMENTS

To an old man who is full of wit and personality and who is the inspiration behind the character of Uncle Billy. Thank you, Billy Fleet.

To a young lady who believed in me and encouraged me through the entire writing process. Thank you, January Levere.

To two kids, now adults, who are and have always been my inspiration. Thank you, Adonis & Athena.

Table Of Content

Chapter 1

The Cat That Went to London: Lesson on Appreciation

"Good afternoon, Ross! School okay today?" Uncle Billy asked his young nephew as he walked through the front door.

Ross Miller is in the sixth grade. He is a dark-skinned, African-American boy who stands about 4 feet tall and is skinny—very skinny. No matter what Ross wears, it always seems to be too big for him. Even his shoes look too big. He has a low cut Afro that looks like his mother cuts his hair. Well—his mom does cut his hair; every second Friday of the month, right after school, she cuts his hair. And he hates it! Oh! How Ross hates that his mother cuts his hair. But, Ross' mother cannot afford to take her son to the barber to get his hair professionally cut—or so she says.

"Why pay for you to get your hair cut when I can cut it for free? Boy, you better stop playing with me." This is what Ross' mother would tell him every time he even hints about getting "a real cut." So for now, Ross gets the comb- and-scissors haircut. It's not the best look, especially on such a skinny kid, but such is life in the Miller household.

Ross' mom—she's a character. Ross' mother is a single mother and

Ross is the only child. Ross' mother was 18 years old when Ross was born. She works hard and does all she can to better herself and provide for Ross. But no matter how hard she tries, she can't seem to get ahead. They live in a small apartment in the inner city, but Ross does not go to school in the inner city. Ross uses his uncle's address and attends school in a distant county—a county where the schools have newer, cleaner, and brighter buildings with much better equipment, science labs, and sports facilities as well as smaller classes with teachers that have more time for the kids. Ross' mother is thankful that her brother allows her to use his address so Ross can attend this much better school.

Ross' mother takes her son to school every morning. She works at a cafeteria in a hospital and the hospital is not too far from Ross' school. She does not have to be at work until 9:00 A.M., so she is able to drop Ross off at the school in the morning before work.

Ross' mom does not get off of work until 6:00 P.M., so every day after school Ross takes the bus to his Uncle Billy's house and stays with him until his mom picks him up.

Uncle Billy is an older man, 67 years old. He is tall, 6'5", and thin, with a muscular, veiny body. When he stands up, his posture is erect, like a swimmer. For a 67-year-old man, he does not lean forward when he walks. His shoulders are squared and his chin is straight. His face is chiseled—defined cheekbones and chin; the hair on his head, though short, is wavy and is silvery white. His eyebrows are full and are streaked with the same silvery white as on his head. His eyelashes are long, almost abnormally long, and they are equally streaked with the silver-white hair.

The contrast of his skin and hair gives him a unique, unforgettable look.

You see Uncle Billy one time and you will never forget him. His skin is a smooth—very smooth—dark leather brown. His skin looks—in a word, healthy, a healthy, Hershey chocolate brown skin tone. And his hands— Uncle Billy has the largest, most veiny hands you have ever seen. Something about his hands is both frightening and gentle at the same time.

A combination of growing up in the south and being in the military molded Uncle Billy's personality. He left home when he was 18 to join the Marines. Uncle Billy has traveled around the world and lived in cities and countries that some people have never even heard of. But for the most part, he is just a country boy, with a country twang in his voice. He never lost it.

Uncle Billy volunteers his time three days a week at a local high school and enjoys fishing and reading. Uncle Billy reads much of anything, but he has his list of favorite books. His favorite author is Napoleon Hill.

Uncle Billy is widowed and has no plans on remarrying. At his age, he feels no need to marry. He enjoys his own company and his own space.

He has an old house that is paid for and is living off the investments he made while he was working. The house is in the suburbs. Uncle Billy is proud that his sister can use his address to allow Ross to attend a better school. He knows that Ross and his mother live in the inner city, where the living conditions are not the best.

Ross gets off the bus and walks through the door to find Uncle Billy in his recliner sitting in the middle of the living room in his small house in the country. It's always so quiet in the country.

Back to the story.

"Good afternoon, Ross! School okay today?" Uncle Billy asked Ross while reading the morning paper he has already read for the day. Uncle Billy likes to stare out of the window, but keeps the newspaper on his lap and his glasses on his nose. Uncle Billy cannot read without his glasses so Ross always knows whether his uncle is actually reading or just holding the paper.

"Eh, school was okay." Ross did not seem too happy today. He was usually more upbeat, like most 13 year olds. But today, something was on his mind. "I wish I lived here with you, Uncle B. I hate where we live."

"Why's that, Ross?" asked Uncle Billy. "There's nothing wrong with where you live."

"Because! Oh my god!" Ross exclaimed. "It's dirty over at Mom's! And the kids at school know I don't live here with you Uncle B. It's embarrassing." Ross plops himself down in the sofa adjacent to Uncle Billy's recliner.

Putting the paper down and taking off his glasses, Uncle Billy looked at Ross. "Well—why don't you clean up your house if you know it's dirty, Boy?"

"Here we go." Ross jumped up from where he just sat down and walked into the kitchen to get a bottle of water. One thing Uncle Billy always had is bottles of water in the refrigerator. He usually didn't have any juice— Uncle Billy was not too much of a sugar guy, but he always had water.

"Well!" Uncle Billy yelled out at his nephew who was now in the kitchen. "How can you say your house is dirty? If your house is dirty, it's because you not cleaning it. Clean it and be happy." Uncle Ross had a way of simplifying matters. He could make a complex situation seem so simple.

"Not that kind of dirty, Uncle B." Ross took the bottle water out of the fridge and walked back into the living room with his uncle. "At mom's house we have roaches, the windows don't close all the way so it's always cold. The kids at school don't like me because of where I live. I just hate it!" Little Ross was getting angry and upset. Tears started to well up in his eyes. He turned back and walked into the kitchen. He tried to hide his tears from Uncle Billy.

Uncle Billy sighed. Seeing that Ross was on the verge of crying, he got up from his recliner and walked into the kitchen where Ross stood with his bottle of water. "Sit down here, Boy." Uncle Billy sat down at the kitchen table and motioned for Ross to sit in the chair next to his. Little Ross was like a high- powered racecar. He could go from 0 to 100 in less than 6 seconds—one second he could seem happy, or least okay, then boom! He was angry and upset. Today was one of those days. And Uncle Billy knew that when Ross got like this, it was time to teach him a life lesson.

"You remember that old nursery rhyme, the one about the cat that went to London?"

"Huh?" questioned Ross. "Uncle B, what are you talking about?" "The cat that went to London, Boy!"

Ross just stared at his Uncle. "You have no idea what I'm talking about do you, Boy?" Uncle Billy asked Ross.

"Uh, no. I don't. No clue, Uncle B." Ross took a drink of his water.

Shaking his head, "What do they teach kids these days?" Uncle Billy was constantly making remarks about how young people today are not learning valuable lessons in school. He believed it was his job to teach his young nephew the valuable lessons of life, the ones the schools were failing to teach the young people today.

"Okay, listen to me, Boy. Listen. There is a nursery rhyme that they used to teach us as kids that goes a little something like this:

"Pussycat pussycat, where have you been? I've been up to London to visit the Queen. Pussycat pussycat, what did you there?

I frightened a little mouse under her chair. Meoww!"

Little Ross just sat there staring at Uncle Billy with a puzzled, confused look on his face. "Um….What did I just hear?"a puzzled Ross said. "That was not a nursery rhyme. Like literally nothing rhymed." Ross was agitated by his uncle's—whatever it was.

"You've never heard that, huh?" asked Uncle Billy.

"No. Can't say that I have, Uncle B. Can't say that I have. But as I was saying…is there any way I can live here with you? You have no idea." Ross was more interested in living with his uncle than learning a lesson about a cat and a queen.

"Wait a minute, Young man. I'm trying to teach you something important. I need you to listen to me now."

"Uncle B. You're talking about a cat that went to London. I am talking about real life. You can't be serious right now? I have problems, real problems. I don't have time to listen about cats and queens in London!" Ross had a way of being feisty when he was upset.

"Now you just listen to me and then, after you listen to me, then we'll talk about you moving in—or not. Is that fair?" Uncle Billy negotiated with his young nephew.

"Okay. Fine." Ross agreed.

"Now, have you ever been to London, Boy?" asked Uncle Billy. "Never."

"Do you know what's in London? Let me guess—you have no idea what's in London?"

Rolling his eyes Ross says, "The Queen?" "See?"

"See what, Uncle B. You said I had to listen to you. You didn't say I had to answer your question."

"Now ain't this some shh---" Another thing about Uncle Billy. He spoke in a way that makes you think he was about to cuss. Maybe he used to curse when he was in the military, but he was mindful and always stopped short of actually saying the curse word. He never cursed around Ross.

"Well—you didn't. You said I just had to listen to you." Ross was being frank.

"Listen and answer me, Ross! You have to listen and answer me, or you can go right on home to your momma and your roaches." Uncle Billy was getting irritated.

"Okay. So what was the question?"

"Do you know what is in London, Ross?" Uncle Billy is almost yelling now.

"I said the queen. The queen is in London." Ross answered his uncle.

"Yes, but what else? What else is in London, Ross?" Uncle Billy was still talking quite loudly.

"I have no idea," admitted Ross.

"If this ain't a mutha—now see? That's another one of your problems right there. You don't know shh—jack.

"In London there are a lot things to see and do. Yes, there is the Queen, but there is also a palace, Buckingham Palace. You ain't never seen anything like the Buckingham Palace. It looks like something out one of those movies you watch all the time except it's real."

"I can't remember watching any movies with a palace in it, Uncle B." Ross interrupted his uncle.

Uncle Billy stopped and just stared at his nephew for a few seconds. He then continued.

"In London, there is this grand church called Westminster Abbey. My Lord! You have to see this church. We call it, 'Ole Abbey.' Magnificence at its finest! Then there is Hyde Park. And then you have to see Kensington Gardens! You will lose your mind seeing the Gardens.

"Then there is the British Museum, Big Ben, the Tower of London. Son, there are amazing things to see and do in London."

"Yeah, sounds like it." Ross was not thrilled at all and wondered why his uncle was talking to him about London when he wanted to talk about moving in with him.

"London is a beautiful place, but here you have this cat, this cat that went to London. And when the cat went to London, it did not see or do any of these wonderful things. Can you believe that, Ross? The cat went to London and didn't do a got darn thing!"

"Amazing." Ross said under his breath.

"But what did the cat do in this nursery rhyme?" Uncle Billy asked Ross. Ross looked up at his uncle with a lost look on his face. "Tell me again?"

Ross could not remember what the cat did in the nursery rhyme that he wanted to forget.

"Pussy cat, pussy cat, what did you there? I frightened a mouse under the queen's chair." Uncle Billy recited that part of the nursery rhyme again.

"That's right!" Ross said, "He scared a mouse."

"He what?" Uncle Billy asked again in what seemed to be a shout.

So Ross yelled out, "He scared a mouse! He scared a mouse under the queen's chair."

"Wow! Can you imagine that? What was wrong with this cat? Out of all the things he could do in London, out of all the things he could see in London, this cat only saw a little rat hiding up under the woman's chair." Shaking his head, "That's a shame. It's a darn shame." Uncle Billy sat back in his chair at the kitchen table like he was disgusted at the cat.

"Yeah. You know, Uncle B. It's not real."

"But it is real! That's my point. And that's what I am trying to teach you, Son. Listen, the moral of this story is, 'you see what you look for.' All that good stuff in London, the cat didn't see. And why didn't the cat see the good stuff?

Because the cat wasn't looking for the good stuff. The cat was looking for the rats. "And that is how it is with you. If you're not looking for the good that is right there in front of you, you'll only see the little rats. Son, you have palaces in your life, right now, at home with your mother. At your school, you have gardens and towers. In your room at your mom's house, you have a Big Ben.

All around you, you have, you have magnificence. Stop looking for rats, Son. Stop looking for rats."

"I'm pretty sure I wasn't looking for rats," quipped Ross. "Roaches, then," said Uncle Billy, "stop looking for the roaches."

"Um, I'm pretty sure I wasn't looking for the roaches either. It's more like they come out looking for me." Ross couldn't help but smile.

Uncle Billy gave Ross a look, then the two busted out in laughter together.

Uncle Billy put his big, wrinkled hand on Ross' head. "You know, Ross, I happen to know something."

"What's that, Uncle B?" asked Ross.

"Your mother, she's a queen—a real life queen. She works so hard for you. Being a single parent is not easy. It's not easy for a man or woman. It's not easy at all." Uncle Billy was deep in thought. Maybe he was thinking of his own mother. Maybe he was thinking of a single father he knew. He paused for a minute and then continued.

"She works with whatever little she has, your mom. Instead of spending money to get money from your father—do you know what I mean by that, Boy?" Uncle Billy stopped to ask this question.

"Not really." Ross answered.

"Child support. Your mother is not hiring some attorney to go chase down your dad to get child support from him. It probably won't work anyhow. She uses what she has to make a better life for you. And I do believe that you have a palace coming, one that is far better than what I'm living in now, I can tell you that. You just need to wait, have a little patience, look at the great things you do have in your life and stop focusing on the things that you don't have."

"So I guess that means—no? I can't come live with you?" asked Ross. "No, you can't come live with me! What's wrong with you, Boy?" Old

Uncle Billy smiled at Ross and then said, "You're the prince of your own palace."

"Uncle Billy!" Ross was not amused.

"Trust me, Ross. If you start appreciating what you have at your own house, you will start to appreciate your own house. I'll tell you what—for the next month, every day, start looking at all the good stuff at your house.

Everything you like and appreciate at your house—your bed, your mother, your pillow—every single thing, start writing it down and why you appreciate it. Can you do that?"

"Sure. And then what?" Ross asked his Uncle because it sounded as though he was trying to make Ross a deal.

"Do that every day for a month and if you still want to move in with me we will talk to your mom and see what happens." Uncle Billy made Ross that offer.

"Really?" Ross was excited.

"Really. But every day you have to write all of the things you actually like about your current home—every single thing—and why you like it." Uncle Billy explained again what Ross had to do for the next thirty days. "You have to look for the good stuff."

"Deal! I will do just that. Where am I supposed to write this stuff down?" asked Ross.

"In a notebook! Where else can you write it down?" Uncle Billy asked the obvious.

"Okay. I wasn't sure if you had a special place you wanted me to write." Ross responded then paused. "Do you—have a notebook I can write it in?" Ross asked.

Uncle Billy nodded his head. "Look over there in the living room in that drawer over yonder. You'll see a blank notebook in there."

"Thanks, Uncle B!" Ross pushed himself away from the table and ran into the living room to grab the notebook.

"Thirty days!" yelled out Uncle Billy.

"Thirty days! Got it. Here comes Mom." Ross ran back into the kitchen where his uncle was sitting. "Thank you, Uncle B."

"Thank me for what, Ross? I ain't given you nothing."

"Oh, but you did. Thank you for—thank you for listening to me—and for the nursery rhyme. I really did enjoy it." Ross smiled a big smile.

"Go on, here." Uncle Billy smiled back at Ross. Ross ran out the front door and to his mom's car.

Thirty days came and went, Ross never mentioned anything about moving in with his Uncle. Ross wrote down everything he liked at his mom's house, everything he enjoyed, everything he was grateful for. Doing this one little assignment changed Ross' perspective on everything. He soon loved his bed and his blue sheets. He loved being with his mother. He loved his video games. He loved coming home after leaving his uncle's house and going to his room. He loved his mother's cooking. He loved waking up and riding to school with his mom.

He had not realized how much he actually loved about living where he was living and soon, the roaches disappeared. He did not know that his uncle gave his mom money for an exterminator. Soon, the apartment was not as cold as it used to be. Ross does not know his uncle helped his mother fix the windows so that they closed all the way.

Life was so much better for little Ross and it was all because he began appreciating what he has. Not just appreciating it in his mind, but literally writing down everything that he enjoyed about his home, his mother, and his life. Writing has a way of revealing things to the subconscious mind. Little Ross learned this lesson by experience. Experiential learning is what it's called. Uncle Billy taught Ross by having him develop knowledge, skills, and values from direct experiences outside of the classroom. This is a lesson Ross will never forget because it is now a part of his life.

Chapter 2

Cultivating and Protecting Your Good Name: Lesson on Reputation

It was late afternoon, about the time Ross would be coming to his uncle's house after school. Ross had had a rough day at school. He stormed through the front door and into the kitchen.

"What's wrong with you, Ross?" Asked Uncle Billy.

Uncle Billy was in the kitchen washing dishes when he turned and noticed a pouting Ross standing in front of the opened refrigerator.

"Get what you need and close the fridge. You letting out all the cold air." Uncle Billy scolded Ross.

Ross rolled his eyes, slammed the fridge door, and stormed into the family room area. Once there, he dropped himself into Uncle Ross' favorite chair, folded his arms, and sat there was an angry scowl on his face. In walked Uncle Billy.

"I know you're not sittin' in my chair!" Uncle Billy said looking surprised.

Ross didn't even bother looking up. He kept staring straight ahead of him with the angry look on his face.

"You can be mad all you want, but you can't be mad and sit in my chair." Uncle Billy said.

Ross didn't budge. And his face expression stayed the same.

"I know you hear me talkin' to you. Get on up!" Uncle Billy began walking towards his young nephew.

Ross sat there for about another two seconds, then jumped up and started to storm back towards the kitchen when Uncle Billy grabbed Ross by the arm.

"Hold on just one minute. Sit yourself down over there....not in my chair!

Sit down over yonder." Uncle Billy motioned for Ross to sit in the love seat adjacent to his recliner.

"I want to go to outside, Uncle Billy." Ross, still with the angry look on his face, stood standing in front of his uncle.

"No, you don't. If you wanted to go outside, you would have been in outside. You wouldn't have been standing in front of the fridge with the door wide open, acting like you were watching TV. And if you wanted to go outside, you wouldn't have come and dropped your narrow behind in my chair. Now sit down over yonder and tell me what's going on with you?" Uncle Billy sat down in his recliner and waited for Ross.

Walking over to the old blue leather love seat that Uncle Billy positioned under the living room window, but not too far from his recliner, Ross plumped down, arms still folded and the angry look still on his face.

"Nothing is going on with me. I'm just tired of people," pouted Ross.

"I get tired of people, too, but I don't get mad about it. What happened?" a concerned Uncle Billy asked.

"Some kids at school..." Ross stopped mid-sentence and his face grimaced even more. He bit down on his bottom lip and squeezed his eyes closed as if he was trying to fight back tears.

"What did some kids do to you, Ross? Talk to me. What's going on?" Uncle Billy was very concerned.

"Some kids at school are going around saying that I'm a liar."

Uncle Billy sat back, relieved that it was not something more serious that what just came out of Ross' mouth.

"Well, are you a liar?" asked Uncle Billy. "No!" shouted Ross.

"Well, why are they saying that you are a liar if you not a liar?" Uncle Billy, as usual, was asking young Ross questions to prove a point.

"I don't know. Jonathan told me that he heard this kid named David tell this other kid named Matthew Mills that he can't believe anything I say because I'm a liar. Then this other kid, John Mudd, signed off on it. I barely even know these guys. Just makes me mad that they will say these things out their mouths about me." Ross was clearly very hurt, but he was opening up now, yet the pain and confusion was still there.

"That sounds like a hot mess!" Uncle Billy said sounding empathetic to Ross' frustration and pain. "And you sure you never lied to nobody, Ross?" Uncle Billy asked with a stern look on his face.

"Nooooo! I already told you that."

"Well, see. There you go lying right there because I know for a fact you done lied to me a few times." Uncle Billy said sarcastically.

"Bye, Uncle B." Ross rolled his eyes in disgust and started to storm off the couch.

"Now wait just one minute, Son!" Uncle Billy motioned for Ross to take a seat back down. "Why are you so bothered by all this? If you know you didn't lie, why be mad? Look at you. Face look like you sucking on a lemon. What's going on with you, Ross?"

"I'm mad because it's not true! I am not a liar! I don't want everyone at school thinking I am a liar when I'm not. I don't want to have a bad reputation in school, Uncle B." Just thinking and talking about it made Ross mad all over again, almost to the point of crying.

"Well, I can understand that." Uncle Billy sat back in his recliner, picked up his magazine and started reading.

"Yeah." Ross sat there expecting his Uncle to say something more. But Uncle Billy didn't say anything more. He just kept to his magazine.

"Okay, Uncle B. What are you doing?" Ross went from anger to agitation at his uncle.

"What does it look like I'm doing? I'm reading my magazine." Uncle Billy didn't even bother looking up at Ross. His face was in his TIME magazine.

Ross looked at his uncle and turned up his lips. "What? You looking at the pictures, Uncle B?"

"What you mean?" Uncle Billy turned to look at Ross.

"You know what I mean. You can't read without your glasses, Uncle B."

Uncle Billy burst out laughing like he it was the funniest thing he'd ever heard. "Haaaaa! I tell you, Boy! I can't get nothing past you! Ha! Ha! You getting smarter by the day! Ha! Ha! My boy! Look at you being all observant! Ha! Ha!" Uncle Billy couldn't stop laughing at that.

The scowl was off of Ross's face now.

"Yeah. So what's up, Uncle B? What have you got to say about all this? You have any words of advice for me? How can I stop this lie from spreading?"

Ross was still upset, but not as upset as before. But he sincerely wanted to know what to do in this situation. Should he be mad? Was he blowing this out of proportion? What was he to do? He had to protect his name and his image.

These were the thoughts that were going through little Ross' head.

"So you got people lying on you. You got people calling you a liar. Yeah, that's tough. Real tough. You don't want your name drug through the mud like that. What did you say that boy's name was? John Mudd?" Uncle Billy was country and you can hear just how country by some of the word phrases he used.

"Yeah, John Mudd. But I don't really know him."

"Well, with a name like John Mudd, what else can you expect?" Uncle Billy put his magazine on the coffee table and sat back in his recliner, crossed his legs, and folded his hands on his knee.

There was a pause; then Uncle Billy said, "You have every reason to be angry, Ross. Every reason."

Uncle Billy stopped again and began staring out the window as if he were trying to remember something. Ross was looking at his uncle because he knew when he started staring out the window like that he was about to say something worth listening to.

"Let me tell you something, Ross." Uncle Billy cleared his throat. "Good name in man and woman, dear my lord, is the immediate jewel of their souls."

Ross stopped his Uncle. "Uncle B…Why…why are you talking like that?" "Like what, Son?" Uncle Billy asked with a surprised, but guilty, look on his face.

"Like that. That's not how you sound when you talk."

"That's my British accent. You didn't know I had a British accent did you, Ross?"

"I still don't." Ross said under his breath. Uncle Billy burst out with his famous laugh.

"You like that though, huh, Boy? Dear my lord. 'lord.'" Uncle Billy was bellowing his "lord" like he was literally from London.

"You like the way that rolls off my tongue? 'Dear my lord.' Ha!"

Ross started giggling then laughing at this uncle, and the two shared in a good laugh at Uncle Billy's British accent.

"So listen to me, now. Listen to me 'dear my lord.'" Uncle Billy smiled a bright smile.

Uncle Billy was smiling then became serious again as he stood up, gazed up into thin air, and transformed, started again accent and all.

"'Good name in man and woman, dear my lord, Is the immediate jewel of their souls.

Who steals my purse steals trash; tis something, nothing! 'Twas mine, 'tis his, and has been slave to thousands.'"

Ross was listening and watching his uncle perform whatever it was he was performing.

"But he that filches—that means steals," Uncle B briefly paused to explain the meaning of filch just in case Ross didn't know or couldn't decipher the meaning on his own and then he continued again.

"'But he that filches from me my good name Robs me of that which not enriches him, And makes me poor indeed. Poor indeed.'"

Uncle Billy ended with a dramatic flourish and sweeping bow.

"Okaaaay. That was weird." Ross didn't know what to make of what he just heard.

"Weird? Did you say that was weird, Ross?" Uncle Billy wasn't expecting Ross to say that was weird.

"I don't know. Maybe it was the accent? I'm not sure. It's not like it was disturbing or anything how you made yourself sound like Idris Elba, but I don't know. Just kinda weird." Ross was being sarcastic.

"Boy. If you don't…" Uncle Billy started shaking his head as he sat back down in his recliner.

"I'm kidding. But…" Ross paused. "Can you say it over again? I didn't get it."

"Why certainly." Uncle Billy said with a smile and in his accent.

"I mean, just—without the Idris voice." Ross could be very witty when he wanted to be.

"What I just got through saying to you was Shakespeare. See? That's what's wrong with this generation today. You people don't know nothin'. You don't read nothing' so you don't know nothin'. All you young people do is stay on your phones and computers. You young people spend way too much time on FaceBook, on Xbook, on Instabook and all those other fake books, and you don't spend time reading real books."

Uncle Billy was getting aggravated by Ross' lack of Shakespearean knowledge.

"Um….I'm almost 100% sure it's X-BOX and Insta-GRAM." There was Ross being sarcastic again.

"You know what I mean!" snapped Uncle Billy. "You into all this online trash and you don't read books! I just quoted Shakespeare and you don't even know. Gave you the accent and everything. Darn shame. Wait until I tell your mother about this."

Uncle Billy sat back and just shook his head.

"Well, now that you mention it—wait, that was Shakespeare?" Ross asked as if he was interested.

"Yes. Shakespeare. 'Good name, dear my lord.'" Uncle Billy gave Ross the accent again.

"Oh, yeah, no. Never heard that one. But go ahead, Uncle Romeo, and tell me what all this means." Ross was on a roll.

"Now would you look at this here? Romeo? Romeo!?" Uncle Billy just shook his head again. "It's Othello. Othello, Boy. Othello, a story about a Black man. Next time I see you, you better have read Othello. I want you to tell me the whole story! You hear me?"

"Yes, Sir." Ross answered and smiled at his uncle.

"Anyway, what I quoted to you means that your name, what people say about you, what people think about you, your reputation—is, it's the jewel of who you are. That means your reputation is the most valuable thing that you can have, Son. You can steal a man's money (and you know how valuable money is) but compared to his good name, it's like trash.

"Everyone has money, loses money, and can make money over and over again. But if you steal a man's reputation, it's like robbing him of everything he has. And when he is robbed of his good name it's taking from him something that does not make the thief rich, but makes the person who was robbed very poor.

"In other words, it's wrong for someone to ruin your name, Ross. It was wrong for those boys to call you a liar and have everyone else believing you are a liar when are not a liar---or at least a habitual liar."

Uncle Billy paused and looked at Ross with slanted eyes. "That's the difference by the way. You don't want people believing you're in the habit of telling lies. No one will believe anything you say if they think you are a habitual liar."

"Exactly! See? That's why I'm so angry! Those boys robbed me! They stole from me, Uncle Billy! I knew you would understand! I knew it! Now what can I do? What can I do to get back my good name? I am not a liar." Ross felt so much better knowing his uncle understood his frustration and pain.

"Well." Uncle Billy sat back, knowing that he had Ross' full attention and that this would be a prime teaching moment.

"The first thing you need to do is realize—this is very important now so listen to me. The first thing you have to understand and realize is that

20

your name, your reputation, is everything. You can't go out there and just do and say anything you want. People label you by what they see you doing and hear you saying. That's your name you messing with when you go out there acting like a fool. No one should see you acting like you don't have good sense! What people see you do and hear you say is how you get a reputation. That reputation can be bad or it can be good, but it's going to be by what people see you do and hear you say. You understand what I'm telling you?"

"Yes, I'm with you, Uncle B." Ross understood clearly.

"Good. That's how you get a name. Make sure you get a good name. In Othello, he is saying that a good name is like a jewel, a precious jewel. In your momma's Bible, you'll see it there too. It says, 'a good name is more desirable than great riches.' Don't take your good name for granted. Protect it."

Ross was listening and thinking—thinking about whether he had been careful in protecting his name, thinking about how he acts around his friends, his teachers, his friends' parents. The wheels in his head were spinning now.

"So, the first thing you have to remember, Ross, is that everything you say and do creates a name. Be mindful of that. Always be aware that your actions and your words define you. Every day, remember that."

Uncle Billy was teaching Ross.

"Okay. I get it. But now that these kids have already robbed me of my good name, what do I do? I am not a liar. No one has heard me or seen me lie, Uncle B. How do I get my good name back?" Ross desperately wanted to know.

"How much money you got saved?" Uncle Billy's question took Ross off guard.

"Huh?" Ross was confused.

"How much money you got saved?" Uncle Billy asked Ross again.

"I don't know? You told me to save and forget about it." Ross answered not knowing why his uncle would be asking him that question when they were talking about something totally different.

"And how long you been saving?" Uncle Billy asked.

"I don't know, Uncle B! About a year." Ross was getting frustrated. "Can we get back to my good name? Please?"

"So how much money do you think you've saved in a year?" Uncle Billy asked.

"Seriously, Uncle B? I don't know. It's not like I have a job. I just save whenever mom gives me money, you give me money, I find money. I don't know. Maybe about $50? I don't know."

Uncle Billy paused. After a few seconds of silence, Uncle Billy continued. "You got all your money in that shoebox you told me about?

"Yes, Uncle B!" Ross was very frustrated now.

"What if I were to tell you that someone stole that shoebox today. How would you go about getting your money back?" Uncle Billy asked Ross.

"What? Oh, no! First off, I would be pissed. Very pissed. I've been saving for a year! And it would take me just as long if not longer to get that money back. It took me a long time to save that money!" Ross was upset just thinking about having to save that money all over again.

"You will have to start saving all over again, huh Ross." Uncle Billy looked at his young nephew. "To get your good name back, you're going to have to start telling the truth all over again."

"Uncle B! I never lied!" Ross stressed to his Uncle.

"Oh, I believe you. Those boys stole your good name though. Now you have to get it back. And the only way you get it back is like the only way you can get your money back if someone stole your shoebox—with time and slowly adding truth back to your good name. And you do that by being sure you never lie again. Tell the truth even if it hurts. It will take some time, but in time, people will know that you are not a liar—if you never lie again." Uncle Billy sat back.

Ross shook his head. It was not the answer he was looking for. But he understood.

"I can do that. But it makes me so mad though." Ross understood that he could really do nothing immediately. He understood that his good name was lost, and it would take time to get it back, and he was angry still.

"Well…" Uncle Billy sat back, "Now that you know how your name is lost, you know what you have to do to get it back. Now, you will be aware.

Before, you might have told a little white lie here and there. Not now. Now, moving forward, you will be honest, brutally honest, because someone stole your good name early in life. Now, you will be known for always telling the truth. I see this whole thing being a good thing."

"A good thing?" Ross asked.

"Oh, yeah. At your age, what? You twelve?"

"Thirteen." Ross quickly corrected his uncle, having just turned 13 the week before.

"At thirteen years old you will now live the rest of your life intentionally being honest. That's a good thing. By the time you're my age, you will be known for telling the truth." Uncle Billy smiled at his young nephew.

"Thank you, Uncle B." Ross said, not sure if he wanted to wait until he was Uncle Billy's age for people to start seeing him as an honest kid, but he understood the message.

"Any time, dear my lord." Uncle Billy said in his accent.

The two enjoyed a good laugh again. By now, Ross' mother was pulling up to pick up Ross to go home.

Chapter 3

My Dog Found My Watch! Lesson on The Power of Thought

"Uncle Billy! Uncle Billy!" an excited Ross came running through the front door of his uncle's house. "Uncle Billy! Guess what just happened!?"

Uncle Billy had fallen asleep in his recliner while reading one of his old books, Outwitting the Devil by Napoleon Hill. The excited young Ross woke up Uncle Billy, who would sometimes enjoy a mid-day nap while reading in his recliner. He was not in a deep sleep so his name being yelled out by Ross didn't startle him awake.

He simply opened his eyes and stared at his young nephew as he came running in through the front door.

"Uncle Billy!" Ross ran up and was now gulping breaths of air as he stood in front of his uncle who was outstretched in the recliner.

"Well—what is it?" Uncle Billy asked Ross, sounding a bit frustrated. Uncle Billy had a way of always sounding frustrated.

"You remember my watch? The one I lost last month? I looked

everywhere for that watch. I thought someone must have stolen it. You remember!!?"

"Yeah, I remember."

Well guess what?" asked Ross.

"You found it." Uncle Billy said in a voice that clearly suggested he wasn't nearly as excited as Ross.

"Yes! I found it! I found it! Check this out, Uncle B. I was out throwing the ball with Jazz."

Jazz is Ross' little Rat Terrier. Ross wasn't allowed to have a dog in his mother's apartment. Ross always wanted a dog. So the agreement between Ross and his mother was Ross could have a dog, but only if his uncle allowed him to keep the dog at his house. Uncle Billy obliged.

Jazz loved to play fetch with a tennis ball. Ross would throw the ball as far as he could and Jazz would ran after it and bring it back to Ross … sometimes, that is if he did not get distracted by another dog, or squirrel, or person. It was a fun game Ross would play with Jazz but the inconsistency of Jazz bringing the ball back made it to where Ross would only play this game with Jazz on evenings he was really bored. Today was one of those evenings.

Ross continued. "I was out in the front yard throwing the ball with Jazz. This one time, I threw it out far as I could throw it—and you know I can throw far."

"Mmmm, mmm. Yeah, you can throw it far. Go ahead." Uncle Billy agreed though still not amused and looking as if he were about to fall back asleep.

"So listen! Jazz took off after the ball, right. I threw it so far, I think he couldn't find it because he was just smelling around, smelling around—just lost. So I yelled out, 'Jazz! Over there! Look over there, Jazz!' He didn't hear me though.

The crazy dog kept smelling where he was smelling. Just crazy. Anyway, the next thing I know, Jazz grabbed something in his mouth and darted off back to me, like he found a rat or something. He started running back to me with something in his mouth that clearly wasn't the ball! When he got to me, guess what was in his mouth?"

Uncle Billy just lay there blinking his eyes as if he was about to fall asleep again any second.

"Hmmm?" Uncle Billy's eyes were closed again.

"I said, 'guess what was in his mouth'? Are you awake?" Ross was trying to contain his excitement.

"I'm awake!" Uncle Billy sat up, rubbing his nose a few times. "What was in his mouth? Your watch?" Uncle Billy asked, still not seemingly amused.

"Yes! OMG! Jazz found my watch!!! Can you believe that? After a month! How did it....Uncle Billy! Are you listening me? This is crazy right? I thought that watch was long gone! Jazz found it! In the yard! How crazy is that? I just can't believe it! I think I need a moment right now! This is crazy!"

Ross was hyper-ecstatic. "Why aren't you excited, Uncle Billy? Do you believe me? Look! My watch." Ross held out his watch for his uncle to see.

"Oh, I believe you, Ross. I believe you," Uncle Billy answered. "I believe you found it and I knew you would find it." Sitting up in his recliner now, Uncle Billy asked, "Do you remember what I told you to do about—about a month ago, right when you lost your watch?"

"No. Oh, wait! Yeah! I remember." Ross said. "You mean when you told me to imagine that I had my watch on my wrist every night before I went to sleep? Is that you mean?" asked Ross.

"That's right. How many nights in a row did you do that for?" Uncle Billy asked his excited nephew.

"Hmmmm…about…I don't know. I think it was a week. I really liked my watch. So it was easy for me to imagine that I found it and that I was

27

wearing it again and was happy." Ross started smiling remembering how happy he would be just thinking about finding his watch again.

"You remember being happy, huh Ross?" Uncle Billy asked. Grinning, Ross chuckled, "Yeah. It helped me go to sleep."

"You were happy you found it, even though you really hadn't found it, huh Ross?" Uncle Billy asked Ross.

Chuckling, Ross answered, "Yeah."

"You were happy, something like you're happy right now, huh Ross?" Uncle Billy, sitting up straight now and wide awake, asked this question, which seemed to cause a light to go off in Ross's head.

"Hey! Yeah!" Ross became shockingly excited as he remembered the exercise his Uncle had him do each night before falling asleep and how happy he would feel as he imagined his watch back on his wrist.

"In my mind, when I was thinking I had found my watch, I was happy!" He paused and thought. "Just like I am now. Exactly like I am now!" He looked at his uncle. "Uncle Billy" pausing because he was at a loss of words, "What just happened?"

"Pull up that chair o' yonder, Boy. Let me talk to you for a minute." Uncle Billy took a deep breath as he thought how he would say what he was about to tell young Ross. "Let me see how I can explain this to you, in a way you can understand."

"Seriously, Uncle B. I'm 13 years old, not 13 months old." Ross quipped sarcastically.

"Ha, ha! I know, Boy. But what I'm about to say—well, most adults don't understand. Or…"

Uncle Billy paused as he looked down at his old wrinkled hands, "Maybe they just don't believe."

"Believe what? Okay, Uncle B, you're starting to act weird." Ross was puzzled by what he was hearing and seeing in his old uncle.

"Just wait, Boy." Rubbing his hands together, taking a deep breath, Uncle Billy proceeded to explain. "I'll say it like this. There are two rules, two laws in this world that you need to know about. One is 'you become what you think about' and the other is 'whatever you meditate on or constantly think about with feeling you create.' These are two laws that must happen. You become what you think about all day long and you create what you think on and feel. If you can get to the point of understanding these two life laws and you apply them, you would will basically have everything you ever wanted for yourself or for someone you care about." Uncle Billy sat back after saying that.

Ross, eye brows raised and a confused look on his face, just stared at his Uncle, not expecting him to say anything like that and not sure what to make of what he just heard, so—he didn't say anything.

"Yeah. Those are laws. Those right there." Uncle Billy said reclining back in a more comfortable position in his favorite chair.

"Okaaaay." Ross said. "I become what I think about and I can create what I think on and feel. All I have to do is—think about it, huh, Unk?

"That's right." Said Uncle Billy. "Well, you have to think and feel it. When you were thinking about having your watch and you were imagining having it again, you felt it. You felt it to the point where you would start smiling. At that moment, the creation process began." explained Uncle Billy.

"Haaaaa haaa!" Ross busted out with a loud laugh. "Uncle B, you've lost your mind."

Uncle Billy looked at his young nephew with wide eyes, shocked by Ross' reaction. After a few seconds of shock he sat back and just shook his head.

"See? That's what wrong with people today. The simple things in life go right over folks' heads and they don't believe. People just don't believe. It's a darn shame." Said Uncle Billy.

"Ah, ha. I can see why." Ross said under his breath.

"What did you say, Boy?" Uncle Billy hadn't quite heard Ross. "I said, 'I can't see why.'" Ross smiled innocently.

"Let me ask you something, Boy. How would you explain your dog finding your watch and bringing it to you? Hmm? Your dog found your watch. How do you explain that?" asked Uncle Billy.

"Mmmm. He smelled it?" Ross said inquisitively.

"Yeah, he smelled it." Uncle Billy said shaking his head and with a little disgust mixed with disappointment in his voice.

"No, I don't know how Jazz found my watch after a month it's been lost. It's weird! I don't even remember my watch being outside. Wait...." Ross paused because he knew he was never outside. "How did my watch get outside? Weird. I don't know and I know is it was outside and Jazz found it. And now I have my watch."

Ross excitedly turned to his watch again and started to put it on his wrist.

"I have my watch, but how or why Jazz found my watch and outside? I don't know how. If you're asking me how did my dog find my watch, I don't know, Uncle B." Ross seemed confused.

"Listen to me, Boy. You have your watch right now because you thought about having your watch—every night for seven nights straight. You thought about having it, you imagined having it, and you felt you actually had it. Whatever you think on and feel you create. It's that simple."

Uncle Billy gave that answer to little Ross directly and then continued. "You see, you are young enough that doubt and disbelief and all that other negative stuff most adults have, have not corrupted your mind yet. It's easier for you to believe. Boy, listen to me, now. Your thoughts turned into a belief and your belief created the situation that brought your watch back. And you didn't even know it." Uncle Billy paused and then started again.

"Do you know what a belief is, Son? A belief is just a thought that your mind has accepted. Did you know that? Write that down. A belief is just a thought that your mind accepts as true." Uncle Billy paused for a few seconds. "I'm going to say that again because you not writing."

"I don't have anything to write with." Ross said.

"Put it in your phone!" Uncle Billy snapped back. "You put everything else in your phone. Listen to me and put this in your phone."

Ross took out his phone and opened his Notes app. Uncle Billy continued.

"A belief is just a thought that your mind accepts. When you think a thought over and over and over and over again, you start to believe that thought. When you add to that thought feeling!—ahhhhh sukki! When you think and feel at the same time, that combination is the beginning of creation, Son. You have the ability to create! And you had no idea." Uncle Billy sat back and shook his head again.

Ross was now sitting on Uncle Billy's sofa that is close to Uncle Billy's recliner. His face looking at his Uncle as if to say, 'You are really sounding a bit crazy right now' but Ross dared not say anything but, "Oh, okay." But little Ross was thinking. This was a simple concept but a concept that seemed too easy and too good to be true.

Uncle Billy continued.

"Let me say it like this right here. When you think about a thing, when you imagine, there it is—imagine. Imagination!" Uncle Billy became excited about using that word imagine. He continued.

"When you imagine something to the point where you feel like that thing is now real, for that minute, no, for those few seconds, you believe that the thing is real. When you feel it, it means you are believing it. Once you get to the point of believing something, remember, believing equals

31

thinking and feeling, right then the creation process starts, and that process will continue until the thing is created."

Uncle Billy stopped talking for a second to allow all what he said to sink into young Ross's head.

"This is deep stuff, Boy. You—you need to be writing this stuff down. Can your watch take notes?"

"Ha, ha. No, Uncle B. My watch can't take notes. Now if I had an Apple Watch maybe, hint, hint." Ross smiled again. But Ross was typing all of this in his phone.

"But now, this is deep. Thanks for sharing. I'm just happy I have my watch. That is for sure. And Jazz found it." Ross paused to think. "And (he paused again) I did think about it every night before I went to bed. I guess, I guess it might just be true."

"Might be true?" Uncle Billy quipped. "Boy, it is true. When you get older you'll see that every single person who is successful, first thought or imagined himself successful and then became successful. That is how successful people create success. That is how people create anything and everything. Shoot! Just look around. Look at your watch. Yeah, look at your watch. Look at it. You think it just came into existence by itself? Huh, Boy?"

"No." Ross answered in a chuckle. "Of course it didn't."

"So how did it come to be a watch? How did your watch become a watch? Do you understand what I'm asking you, Boy?" Uncle Billy had a way of talking extremely loud when he was excited—almost at a shouting level.

"What was your watch before it was a watch, Ross!?" Uncle Billy was trying to get Ross to think on his own—but seemed frustrated in asking the question.

"I don't know!" Ross yelled back, just because his Uncle was yelling.

"What was the watch before it was a watch? How about you tell me, Uncle B?" Ross said.

"I'm asking you, Ross!" Uncle Billy wanted Ross to think.

"I guess it was parts? I don't know. A little hand, a big hand, glass, leather." Ross chuckled as he gave his answer.

"That's right! Parts. Your watch was parts. All watches are made of parts. But parts are not a watch, are they, Ross? Someone had to put the parts together before it became a watch. And someone had to think about a watch, how it worked, what it would look like, maybe even picturing it on a little skinny, black wrist like yours, before they sat down and started putting it together. The watch didn't just become a watch on it's own, did it, Ross?" Uncle Billy asked his nephew.

"Uh, no?"

"No! The watch didn't just say, 'Hey parts. Come together and make me.' You understand what I'm telling you, Boy?" Uncle Billy was sitting up straight now. "The watch came together when and only when somebody put it together. And the only way a person could have put it together was first thinking about it already put together. The watch first existed in somebody's mind, and then the parts were put together and became a watch." Uncle Billy leaned back in his chair and allowed that to sink into Ross' head.

"Okay. Well, of course. Someone made the watch. That person planned it out first and then he put it together. I get it." Ross said it in a way that was obvious.

"Exactly! He thought about it, over and over and over again, until he felt that it could be made, then he made it. And that is what happens with everything. It's the law of belief. Believe a thing and the thing begins to become real—if you persist in the thought. The problem is, people stop believing." Uncle Billy settled himself back down.

"That all sounds so—so simple, Uncle B. So if I believed Ma had a big house and I believed we weren't living in that old dirty apartment, what you're saying is we would be living in a big house? Is that what you're telling me?" Ross gave Uncle B the side look with his lips turned up.

"Yup." Uncle Billy answered while sipping on his now cold tea.

Ross just sat and stared at his uncle. "Okay, Uncle B. Then I'm going to start thinking about that every night before I go to sleep?"

"That's right. You keep thinking about that every night before you sleep and watch what happens." Uncle Billy assured Ross. Uncle Billy continued. "See, it's what some people call—oh, what is it called?" Uncle Billy could not seem to remember. Then it hit him. "The strangest secret! That's what they call it. That's what it is. The strangest secret."

"What's the strangest secret?" asked Ross puzzlingly.

"What we talking about, that's what." Uncle Billy answered matter of fact. "I'm asking you." Ross was confused.

"I'm telling you," answered Uncle Billy. "But you didn't tell me," snapped Ross.

"I didn't tell you what?" Asked Uncle Billy.

"You didn't tell me what the strangest secret was." Ross said. "I just told you." Responded Uncle B.

"You know what—never mind, Uncle B."

"See? That's what's wrong with you children today. You don't listen. Look here. The greatest—

"Strangest." Ross interrupted. "What you say, Boy?"

"Strangest. You said the strangest secret, not the greatest secret." Ross answered.

"Boy!" Uncle Billy just stared at little Ross. smirk.

"Sorry, Uncle. Go ahead. Tell me about the strangest secret." Ross smiled a

"The strangest secret. Oh, yes. The strangest secret. You know what the strangest secret is, Boy?"

"No. I…I'm waiting for you to tell me."

"The strangest secret ever told is that you become what you think about—all day long. That's it right there." Uncle Billy sat back, proud of himself for remembering and proud that he was able to share this important idea. He went on.

"Thinking-and-believing is the most important thing you can do, Son."

Little Ross loved when his uncle called him "son." Without his father present in his life, hearing "son" made him feel—loved and wanted. There is something about a man telling a young man loving words.

Uncle Billy continued, "You become what you think about. Everything about you is the sum total of what you think and believe of yourself. If you are weak, you must believe you are weak. You have to. That's the only way you become weak.

The best basketball player to ever live—" "LeBron James!" Ross quickly interrupted.

"No, Boy!" Uncle Billy shot back. "Michael Jordan. Michael Jordan is the best basketball player to ever live." Uncle Billy paused and looked at Ross like he was crazy for saying LeBron James. He continued.

"In an interview, Michael Jordan, the greatest basketball player to ever live, was asked what he is thinking about when he's out there on the court. Jordan said, 'that there is no one who can stop me.' Michael Jordan thought that no one could stop him and guess what? No one could stop him. There is a very old poet, Virgil— look him up—he wrote, 'they succeed because they think they can.' Let me tell you this, Boy—When you think, you believe, and once you start believing, you start creating. Start thinking, Ross. Start believing. Does that watch have an alarm?" Uncle Billy asked Ross.

"Of course, Unk!" Ross was still excited about his watch Jazz found.

"Good! Set it for every hour and every time you hear it go off, stop and make note of what you are thinking about right when the alarm goes off. When you hear the alarm, stop right then and write down what was on your mind the second that alarm set off. This will help you monitor the crazy things that are going through your little head. And so when you catch yourself, you can then start intentionally thinking of something worthwhile, something good. Are you listening to what I'm telling you?"

"I'm hearing you, Uncle B." Ross was listening—and thinking. "But how, Uncle B? How does this work?"

"Well, it's a law. You know what a law is, right? Whatever you think about…" Uncle Billy paused for a few seconds, "constantly….you have to think on it all the time, what you think about all the time you become that thing. So how did it happen? You thought about becoming the owner of your lost watch, didn't you?

Didn't you, Son." Uncle Billy was asking his nephew this question to keep him engaged.

"Yes, Sir. Every night." Ross answered.

"And what happened? You became the owner of your watch. See? It's a law. Like gravity. If you climb up to the top of the house and jump off, guess what? You'll come down. You won't go up. That's law. It's the same type of law. You become what you think about. That's it. Write that down in your phone. You become what you think about. Write!"

Ross typed this nugget in his phone.

"So think about only good things, Son. Only good things. For as much as you can." Uncle Billy paused again and then continued. "You have to control your thoughts if you want to control your life, Ross. You have to." Uncle Billy reclined back. "Now go on and get out of here. I need to take a nap."

Ross left his uncle, but the idea of thinking and becoming, the idea of controlling his thoughts, the idea of believing began to stick with him.

Chapter 4

Control Who You Become: Lesson on Choosing Friends

Today was not a typical day.

A typical day was Ross coming to his uncle's house right after school, which was typically around 3:30 P.M., and waiting for his mom to pick him up around 6:30 P.M. This was the routine Monday through Friday, every day of every week. But today was different.

Today, Ross' mother dropped Ross off at Uncle Billy's house at 8:00 in the morning instead of taking him directly to school. At Ross' school they had what was called teacher workdays. This was a day when the teachers had to come to the school to work, but the kids did not or could not come to school. Since Ross' mother had to go into work Monday through Friday and since she did not want Ross staying at home by himself, on this day Ross' mother took him to her brother's house—Uncle Billy's house.

Ross was not too excited about this. He wanted to stay home. He was 13 years old and felt he was old enough to stay home by himself. Plus, he wanted to hang out with some kids in his neighborhood, but that was the very reason his mother did not want him staying at home alone. The neighborhood kids, according to Ross' mom, were not the kind of kids Ross needed to hang out with.

"Thank God they did not go to your school" is what Ross' mother would often say.

Ross had seen the boys playing basketball or just hanging out around the local playground. The way his life was set up, he never had time to play with the kids in the neighborhood. Every single day outside of school when he had more than a couple of hours of free time, Ross was at his uncle's house. His mother was protective, very protective. She did not want him hanging out with those "street boys" or "hood rats," as she would sometimes call them.

So after school, it was Uncle Billy's house, and every weekend it was church, his grandmother's house, and at home doing chores and homework. This was Ross' life.

Ross did not go to his uncle's house much on the weekends. His mother figured that going there every day after school was enough for Ross. Besides, it was her way of giving her brother a break. After school five days a week was enough time.

Ross' mother did not want to be a burden on anyone. No way. She was a strong, independent woman. She did not want to overload her brother— not that her brother would mind. Uncle Billy enjoyed the time Ross would come over, but no one could ever tell. Uncle Billy never voiced how much he enjoyed his nephew. He never complained, but he never said he actually wanted the time with Ross.

Ross was indifferent. He didn't mind going to his uncle's house, but today, he wanted to stay home. All the kids were out of school, and he wanted to go hang out with the boys. The fact that he could not left Ross feeling a bit salty. So he was not in the best of moods when he was dropped off at his uncle's house.

Ross' mother was running late for work that morning. Ross is usually up and ready for school every morning by 7:00 A.M, but this morning, he was moving a bit slower. He didn't know what he should wear. He didn't feel like eating breakfast, but his mom wanted him to eat before he went to his uncle's— she didn't want him eating up all her brother's food. "You not going over there hungry—you better put something in your belly before we leave." Ross' mother did not play. Ross knew that and did not think twice about talking back. If he even looked like he was going to say something in opposition to his mother, his mother would snap.

Now Ross' mother would not hit Ross, not now at age 13, but she didn't have to. When Ross was five, six, seven, and even eight years old, Ross would get it—oh, would he get it. And all those backhands and smacks upside the head years prior were traumatic enough to where Ross would not test his mother at age 13. Ross' mother had him trained—in a way like Pavlov's dogs.

For those who might not be familiar, there was a Russian psychologist— his name was Ivan Pavlov. Pavlov was researching how his dogs would salivate when it came time to being fed. He discovered that food caused his dogs to salivate, meaning they would produce saliva or spit in their mouths. Pavlov used a metronome to carry out this experiment. A metronome is a clocklike device that clicks on pace to help musicians play at a certain speed—Pavlov used one of these metronomes to condition the dogs.

Pavlov would turn one of these metronomes on right before he fed the dogs. After a while, as soon as the dogs would hear the metronome, they would begin to salivate because the dogs knew what would come next— the food. So all Pavlov had to do was put on a metronome and the dogs would salivate.

Not comparing Ross to a dog, but this is how it was for Ross and his mother. In those early years, Ross' mother would give him a look and then smack him upside the head every time he would misbehave. So now, at age 13, all she had to do was give him the look and Ross would settle himself down and quick.

So this morning, Ross didn't want to eat, but his mother told him he had to put something in his stomach so he would not be going to his uncle's house hungry. She gave him a look and so Ross quickly grabbed a bagel and an apple. But he was still moving slower than usual. His slow movements made his mother on the verge of being late.

When Ross' mother pulled up to Uncle Billy's driveway, she did not have time to get out and speak with her brother. She told Ross to tell Uncle Billy she said 'thank you' and to be sure and behave himself while he was there for the day. She kissed her son on the forehead and told him, "Hurry up and get out.

Momma got to get to work." As soon as Ross stepped out of the car with his book bag, bagel and apple in hand, his mother backed out of the driveway and zipped off to work.

Ross slowly walked up to his uncle's house and rang the doorbell. Uncle Billy took his time to come to the door. He opened the front door, looked down at Ross and said, "You a bit early, ain't cha, Son?"

Ross wasn't in the mood. Ross just looked up at his uncle, used his left hand to push the door further open, and he just walked by his uncle to go into the house.

"And good morning to you too." Uncle Billy said to his young nephew as he just walked by him without saying a word. Uncle Billy could tell something was wrong.

"So you don't speak when you come to my house in the morning?" Uncle Billy asked Ross.

"Uncle B, I'm tired." Ross slipped the book bag off his shoulder, dropped it on the sofa in the family room, and took a bite out of his bagel as he walked into the kitchen.

Uncle Billy closed the front door and started walking to the kitchen to finish cooking his own breakfast. When he reached the kitchen, Ross was sitting at the table. "Well I'm tired too, but at least I can say good morning." Uncle Billy said to Ross as he walked to the stove.

Ross just rolled his eyes, pulled out his bagel and slowly started eating.

"So what has gotten into you this morning anyway, Ross? I know my house is not that bad."

"It's not your house, Uncle B." Ross answered. "Why can't I stay at home? I'm 13 years old now. Clearly, I am old enough to stay at home by myself. She's treating me like I am 3 not 13."

"Why do you want to stay home by yourself? What can you do at home that you can't do here? Everything you have at home, you have here. I don't see why you have to be all sour about it." Uncle Billy was scrambling his egg whites as he talked to Ross, his back facing towards Ross.

"You just don't get it. I want to be alone sometimes." Ross said.

"Well, take your lil' narrow behind to the guest room then. Ain't nobody going to bother you up there. You'll be good and alone." Uncle Billy smiled at his nephew while he walked the scrambled eggs to the kitchen table where Ross was sitting. After he scraped his eggs to his plate, he walked to the kitchen sink, put the frying pan in the sink, and then walked back to the kitchen table and sat down right next to Ross.

Ross just sat with a look of disgust at his uncle. "I don't mean alone, alone. I mean alone with the guys in the neighborhood." Ross explained to his uncle.

"Oh!" Uncle Billy put a fork-full of scrambled egg whites into his mouth.

"You want to hang out with the big boys in your neighborhood. I see. You should have just said that." Uncle Billy was sounding sympathetic with his little nephew.

"Exactly! I never get to play with the kids right where I live. How crazy is that?"

Uncle Billy was tearing into his breakfast. "Well...wait a minute." Uncle Billy got up from the table to go into the back pantry to get his bottle of Vitamin Water. Uncle Billy always had to have a bottle of sugar free Vitamin Water with this breakfast. Uncle Billy grabbed the bottle of Vitamin Water from the pantry just off the back of the kitchen, then walked back in and sat down to his breakfast and to Ross.

"Well, did you tell your mother?" Uncle Billy asked his question then took a big gulp of his vitamin water.

"Tell my mother what?" Ross was getting annoyed from watching his uncle eat and drink. Ross hated to hear his uncle eat and drink. It sounded so---ugh.

"Tell your mother what you told me." Uncle Billy put another fork full of eggs into his mouth. "No."

Uncle Billy was smacking on his food for a bit then said, "Why not?" He then took another big gulp of his vitamin water.

Ross looked at his uncle from the corner of his eyes. "Do you want to just talk when you're finished eating? I mean. It's not that it's annoying listening to you chew like a horse; I just figured you'd want to enjoy your breakfast alone. I can wait; it's not a problem." Ross could be sarcastic when frustrated.

Uncle Billy just ignored the sarcasm. Or maybe he didn't even catch it. "Mmmm." Uncle Billy still had food in his mouth. "No, no. I'm fine. Go 'head and tell me. Why didn't you tell your mother? It sounds like a reasonable request. You just say…" Uncle Billy put another fork full of eggs into this mouth.

"Say, 'hey mom. I want to stay home so I can meet the guys in my neighborhood.'" Uncle Billy sat back and finished chewing his breakfast while he looked at Ross.

Ross stared at his uncle for a few seconds and then said, "Yeah, that won't work. She does not think the guys in my neighborhood are the type of kids I should hang out with. It's almost racist."

Uncle Billy was just taking another gulp of his vitamin water when he almost choked. "Boy!" Still coughing and chocking. "Did you just call your mother a racist? Now, that is the silliest and funniest thing I've ever heard. Racist! Haaaa!" Uncle Billy was laughing so hard his eyes started to water.

Ross was not laughing. "I did not call her a racist. I said it's almost racist. She does not want me hanging out with a certain type of person just by the way they look. How is that not racist?" Ross reasoned.

Uncle Billy caught his breath and got himself together after hearing what he thought was the most funny, absurd statement he'd ever heard in his life.

After getting himself together, he put both hands on the kitchen table and said, "Well, first off, I don't think your mother has any beliefs about the boys' race in your neighborhood. What race are these boys we talking about?" Uncle Billy stopped to ask this question.

"They're black." Ross answered.

"Right. I don't think your mother believes that these boys are a certain way because they are black. She's black. Whatever it is or whatever reason your mother has for not wanting you to play with these boys, if that is even true, has nothing to do with race. Has she ever told you she don't want you playing with black people?"

"No." Ross answered.

"It's just these people?" Uncle Billy pressed the issue. "Yeah, I guess." Ross answered.

"Right. So it cannot be about race. Now if it is true that your mother does not want you hanging out with these boys, I am sure she has a reason, and I am sure that reason has nothing to do with race. Why do you suppose she does not want you hanging out in the streets with these boys?" Uncle Billy asked Ross.

"I don't know. Because it is a bad neighborhood and she assumes that they are bad. I have no idea, honestly."

"Well, wait a minute, now. How do you even know there are boys in your neighborhood your age?" Uncle Billy seemed to be confused.

"Because I see them hanging outside when I come home from your house after school." Ross answered.

"Every day?" Uncle Billy asked.

"Pretty much." Ross answered.

"So maybe your mother thinks they hang out in the streets too much and so she does not want that type of influence around you." Uncle Billy now finished with his breakfast, stood up from the table and took his plate and fork to the sink. He ran water over his dishes, poured some dish detergent on the dishes to let them soak, then he walked back to over where Ross was sitting at the table. "Let's move on into the living room." Uncle Billy beckoned his nephew to follow him into the living room. "Sit down and let me talk to you for a minute."

Uncle Billy sat down in his blue recliner and waited for Ross to sit down and get situated. He started with, "Let me share a wise old saying with you. It goes like this, 'a man is known by the company he keeps.'" Have you ever heard that before?" Uncle Billy stopped to give Ross a chance to answer.

"Can't say that I have, Uncle B. Can't say that I have."

"Well, 'a man is known by the company he keeps' means that the people you hang around with, spend most of your time with, literally define who you are.

"There's another saying: 'Show me your friends and I will tell you who you are.' Or 'show me your friends and I will show you your future.' Your momma's Bible says something like, 'he that walks with wise men will be wise, but...'"

Uncle Billy paused to try to remember then said, "a companion of fools will be destroyed.' What all these words of wisdom teach us, Son, is that the people you choose to surround yourself with, influence you so much that you become just like these people. If every day you come home from school and you see these boys hanging around outside, just hanging— doing nothing but hanging out—then, if you start hanging around these kids pretty soon you will be outside every day hanging around doing nothing. Your mom is just protecting your future, Ross."

"Mmmmm." Ross sat quiet for a minute. He was thinking. For a 13-year- old Ross was a deep thinker. "So if the boys were outside doing something else—say they were outside and they all had books in their hands and they were in a circle reading books, are you saying Mom would be okay with me staying at home and hanging outside reading with them?"

"Oh, definitely! One hundred percent yes. She would see and, I am sure, appreciate the fact that the boys were doing something productive. She would see that and say to you, "Why not get to meet those boys in the neighborhood? They seem like some really nice boys. Your mother…she likes boys who read."

"I'm sure she does." Ross responded.

"Listen. There is an important lesson here. You can, in a way, control who you become. You want to be an athlete? Start hanging out with the athletes—if they will let you."

"Wait. What do you mean, if they will let me? Why wouldn't they?" Ross asked.

"It's hard to fit in with athletes if you're not an athlete yourself. But if you can fit it, you'll fit in." Uncle Billy explained.

"Well, I am one of the fastest kids in my class, Uncle B."

"That's great! Or not really. Can you beat me in a race yet? I don't think so." Uncle Billy was messing around with Ross, even though he really might be able to beat his young nephew in a foot race.

"Yet, Uncle B? Are you being serious right now?" Ross asked his uncle. "Listen. If you want—listen to me now—if you want to be an athlete, start hanging around with all the athletes at your school, start getting acquainted with other athletes, spending the majority of your time with athletes and pretty soon you will be just like the athletes, or at least have the mindset of an athlete. Their athletic influence will rub off on you.

"If you want to be a straight-A student. Guess what? You should start hanging around all the straight-A students in your school. Introduce yourself, be friendly, invite them to sit down at lunch with you, ask to sit down with them— do whatever you can to be friends with as many straight-A students as you can and soon you'll be a straight-A student. Any type of person you want to be, befriend that type of person and you'll be that person." Uncle Billy sat back.

"Really now?" asked Ross. "So what if I wanted to be rich? Does it work for being rich too?"

To be so young, Ross seemed overly concerned with money and being rich. Maybe it was because his mom did not have much money and he thought they were struggling financially. He always asked questions about money.

"Absolutely! You will never see a rich man with poor friends. Oh, the rich man will have a lot of poor people in his life, but they won't be his close friends, not all of them. He'll have a lot of poor freeloaders. But a rich man won't have poor best friends. Nope. It ain't happening.

"The surest way to be rich is to have at least three rich friends, and I mean close friends, not the ones you can't call up and hang out with any time you want. It works with any kind of person."

Uncle Billy stopped talking for a minute, looked for his book that was on the coffee table, and picked up while asking, "You want to be a clown?"

Ross squinted his eyes and said, "Who wants to be a clown, Uncle B?"
"Some of you young people want to be class clowns. Cutting up and

telling jokes all day. Funny as can be. You want to be a comedian?" Uncle Billy put his glasses on that was laying on the coffee table.

"No?" Ross answered in almost a question like tone.

"Okay then. I was going to say. If you want to be a clown, find all of those clowns in your school and hang out with them. They're funny alright. They're cool. People like to laugh. Girls like funny guys. When you get into high school, remember what I'm telling you. You'll see clowns. And if you want to be a clown, hang with the clowns. But after high school, guess what? They will still be clowns. And unless they land a movie gig being a clown—like some of these people you see on TV now---what's that little boy's name be in all those movies?" Uncle Billy looked over at Ross from over the rim of his glasses.

"I have no idea who you're talking about." Ross never even bothers trying to think about the person his uncle is trying to name.

"You know who I'm talking about. Little, short black guy. High voice." "Are you talking about Kevin Hart?"

"There you go!" Uncle Billy remembered his name now. "Don't get me wrong. Clowns can make money, too. But you have to be a big-time clown. My point is, you can be whatever it is you want to be if you only wisely choose your friends. Whatever you want to be. You just have to choose who you spend the majority of your time with."

"Well, as of right now, I spend the majority of my time with you, Uncle B."

"Bingo! You destined for greatness then, Boy. Ha! Ha!" Uncle Billy was smiling from ear to ear with that one as he turned back to his book and turned a page.

Ross subtly rolled his eyes. "I want to be rich, Uncle B. Where do I find rich kids?

"Who said you have to find rich kids? I said you have to have rich friends.

Most kids are not rich. Their parents are rich. You want to find rich people— broaden your horizon, Boy. Go find you some rich people and befriend them."

Uncle Billy clarified that one little nuance—not kids only, but people, adults included.

"How is a 13-year-old supposed to befriend a rich grown-up, Uncle B?" Ross asked.

"Just like you befriended me." Uncle Billy said matter of factly. "You're not my friend, Uncle B. You're my uncle."

"Well, ain't that a—I should call your momma right now." Uncle Billy started patting his pants pockets as if he was looking for something. "Where's my phone?"

"Seriously, Uncle B?" Ross asked.

"You know how many uncles don't allow their nappy-headed nephews to come to their house?" Uncle Billy was about to teach Ross another lesson. "People believe a friend is someone who has to be your age. You don't have to be the same age, or color, or size to be friends with someone. Just be friendly and when that person is friendly with you, the two of you develop a…a mutual affection. Then you're friends. You can be family and you can be friends. You my nephew but you also my friend." Uncle Billy shook his head.

"This boy said, 'you my uncle.'" Uncle Billy was talking to himself. "Sorry about that, Uncle B. When you put it like that, you are my friend."

Ross smiled at his uncle. "Hey Uncle B., you mind if I grab one of your Vitamin Waters from the back?"

Uncle Billy looked up at his young nephew who was now standing up ready to walk into the kitchen to grab the water. "You asking as a friend or a nephew?" Uncle Billy asked without a smile on his face so that Ross did not know whether he was being serious.

"Which one do I have to be for the answer to be yes?" The two started laughing.

"Boy, go on." Uncle Billy shook his head, hoping that his young nephew caught on to this important lesson—you literally have the power to be who you want to be by simply choosing whom you befriend.

If only more young people realized this and knew this, Uncle Billy thought. Shoot, if only older people realized this and knew this. Birds of a feather flock together. People need to decide what type of bird do they want to be. Once you decide, then go find this type of bird and choose to flock with them. And in deciding what type of bird you want to be, also choose what type of bird you do not want to be. Once you make that decision, stay clear of all people who match this type. Shun the people you know you don't want to be anything like. If not, you will inevitably be them.

Chapter 5

Black History: A Lesson on Black History

"Hey Uncle B!" Ross walked into the front door of his uncle's house after the bus dropped him off from school. The front door was sometimes open because Ross's uncle knew Ross would be coming to his house exactly around 3:45 PM every day.

"Uncle B!" Ross walked straight back into the kitchen looking for his uncle and found him washing off some dishes over the kitchen sink.

"Hey Uncle B. We're off from school on Monday so Mom is going to bring me over in the morning. I was wondering if I can bring my X-Box with me when I come over."

Uncle Billy had on his white, sleeveless t-shirt and some black denim pants. It was cold outside, but warm enough inside of Uncle Billy's house to where he did not have to have on a shirt.

Uncle Billy turned the water off and asked Ross, "Why you ain't got school on Monday? You just had some days off last month. They cutting back on school days now?" Uncle Billy dropped his dish-drying towel of the edge of the sink and made his way towards his living room.

"No, Uncle B. It's President's Day. It's a holiday." Ross answered. "Since when they give you all a holiday for the Presidents?" Asked Uncle Billy.

"Since there's been presidents, I guess. But is it okay for me to bring my X-Box. I'll make sure all of my homework is done first." Ross was focused on his games.

"You know what this month is, don't you boy." Uncle Billy asked his nephew.

"It's February." Ross paused for a minute. He was not sure if his uncle was ignoring him on purpose or if he just wasn't paying him much attention. So he waited before he asked again. "So—is it okay?"

"What else is it, Ross?" Uncle Billy sounded frustrated.

"Uncle B! What do you mean what else is it?" A puzzled Ross answered, getting frustrated himself.

"What else besides February is this month, Boy?"

Ross stared at his uncle, shook his head and said, "Valentine's Day? Can I please bring my X-Box on Monday? Please."

"Now ain't that some---Valentine's Day? Valentine's Day?" Uncle Billy could not believe what he just heard his young nephew say. "I'm speechless! I am just dog gone speechless. I asked you what month is this month and you give me a day. And you go to school?" Uncle Billy sincerely began to feel and look depressed.

"I'm just messing with you, Uncle B. I know what this month is. It's Black History month. Duh." Ross was being silly.

"You didn't know." Uncle Billy was not amused.

"I did know." Ross's voice went up in pitch as he explained to his uncle that he knew all along that February was Black History month.

"Well what you know about black history?" Uncle Billy walked to his recliner, sat down, and reclined back to get comfortable.

Ross rolled his eyes and sighed under his breath, "Here we go."

"Go on and tell me. What you know about black history, Boy?" Uncle Billy crossed his feet and folded his hands on his lap.

"I know….I know…". Ross paused to think. "I know Martin Luther King had a dream and then gave a speech about it." Ross answered feeling proud of himself.

Uncle Billy just sat there looking at his nephew—half in amazement and half in disgust.

Shaking his head and frowning Uncle Billy said, "Sit down in that chair.

Right there." Uncle Billy was about to start school his young nephew.

"Uncle B, seriously?" Ross asked with disbelief. He did not want a lecture right now.

"Sit!" Uncle Billy said with a stern voice.

"Do you know why there is a black history month, Boy?" Uncle Billy asked.

Ross sat down with an uninterested face, sighed and then said, "No." "Now see!?!" Uncle Billy exploded.

"See what, Uncle B?" Ross snapped.

"That is what I am talking about. They don't teach ya'll nothing in these schools! That is the first thing they should have taught you. Listen here—black history month started out as black history week. Write this name down. Put it in your phone. Don't you ever forget this name, Ross." Uncle Billy stopped and was looking at his nephew.

Ross looked up at his uncle. He was looking down at his shoes for some reason until the silence caught him off guard. "Okay. I won't."

"Write it down!" Uncle Billy shouted out. "With what?!" Ross somewhat shouted back.

"Your phone! You write everything else down in there. Use your phone!" "Okaaaaay." Ross pulled his phone out and opened up his notes app. "Now." Uncle Billy continued. "The name I want you to write down is

Carter Woodson. Let me hear you say it. Say his name!" This is how Uncle Billy taught—by having his nephew repeat names or phrases or whatever he was trying to teach.

"Carter Woodson." Ross said with a sigh.

"Carter Woodson. That's right. In 1926, Carter Woodson was a black man who graduated from Harvard University. A black man graduating from Harvard in the early 1900s? Are you kidding me? That Carter Woodson! Ha!

Ha!" Uncle Billy laughed with pride and excitement as he started talking about the achievements of Carter Woodson.

Uncle Billy continued. "Carter Woodson is the guy who started it all. That's right. In 1926, Carter Woodson started Negro History Week. After a while, it became Black History Month. But it all started with Carter Woodson. Did you write that name down, Boy?"

"Yeah...I mean, yes, Sir." Ross was still not amused and did not want to be lectured after school. "Is there anything else?"

"Yeah, there is a lot more else. You don't know nothing about the history of colored folks, do you, Boy?" Uncle Billy didn't know where else to go with his history lesson because he did not think his young nephew new anything at all.

"I do. I know a lot actually." Ross said matter of factly. He realized he was not getting out of this so he might as well make it fun. "Okay. I know that—I know that the late great Michael Jackson was actually a black man." Ross said proudly.

Uncle Billy looked at his young nephew with a surprised look on his face.

He didn't know whether to laugh or cry. So he just took a deep breath and stared---speechless.

"What?" Asked Ross.

Uncle Billy was not even going to bother responding to that. But that did remind him of a musical black history fact.

"Did you know that America's first original music was the Negro spiritual?" Uncle Billy asked Ross.

"What a Negro spiritual?" Ross asked as though he really did not know.

"Boy!" Uncle Billy jumped up and started looking for his magazine to roll up and bop Ross on the head with it.

"I'm joking, Uncle B!" Ross burst out laughing.

"Don't play with me, Boy. Don't you play with me!" Uncle Billy was hot! And Ross could not stop laughing. Ross loved to get his uncle wired up. It was just so easy.

Uncle Billy sat back down, caught his breath, and started back again. "Before rock and roll, before country music, before R & B, before rap, it was the Negro Spiritual. The songs the Negros would sing out in the planation--the melody. Before that, the music in America was European music, they called them European classics and Anglo-ballads. But the original music, outside of the Native Indians, was music from slaves—the Negro Spiritual.

"Are you being serious, Uncle B." This stuff was beginning to interest Ross.

"Oh, yeah. See, you need to know this stuff. And it's a shame that they don't teach you this in school. The Negro spiritual. America's first original music. And you know what else? There will never again be any new Negro spirituals. Oh, you have people singing the Spirituals and performing the songs, but there will never be a new Negro Spiritual. Never."

"Why not, Uncle B? There are still black people." Ross questioned. "There may be black people, but there are no black slaves---at least not like there was back then. The Negro spiritual was born, was born in the souls of enslaved people living in a free world. Unspeakable pain was the composer of the Spirituals. Today, we can never know of this pain. We can never feel the sting of slavery. That type of music-making is now extinct. Blood, sweat, and tears in literal slavery gave birth to song. Moans turned into sweet-sounding melody. Real soul music. That's what it was. Soul music."

Uncle Billy sat back and stared out the window that was to the left of his recliner. He was deep in thought. Ross looked at his uncle and wondered what could he be thinking about. What was it about slavery that made him stop and stare like this. But the fact about the Negro spiritual intrigued young Ross.

"Wow, Uncle B. That's kinda cool. Well, not cool. I just never thought of it like that. I don't know many Negro spirituals, but it makes me want to go back and listen to them. I wonder how many Spirituals there are." Ross said.

Uncle Billy was still staring out of the window—deep in thought. It was as though he did not hear Ross. Or maybe he did.

"Slavery must have been really bad, huh Uncle B?" Ross was trying to get his uncle talking again.

Uncle Billy slowly turned back to his nephew.

"Bad? Really Bad?" Uncle Billy asked and then paused. There was silence.

"Our African descendants should have never made it out alive. They should have all died." It looked as though Uncle Billy's eyes were welling up with tears. "You don't even know." Uncle Billy paused again. Looking down at his hands he said, "Scientists and doctors marvel at the African slave. With all the foreign diseases in this county, diseases the African did not have in their country, no medical treatment, no nothing---scientist agree that they should have all died within the first year of coming to this country. They overcame diseases and malnourishment. That's why I get on you about how you eat."

"Why is that, Uncle B?" Ross asked.

"Because that food was slave food. You not a slave." Uncle B was referring to some of the foods he snapped at Ross's mother for giving Ross one day.

"Everything the master didn't eat was given to the slaves to eat." Uncle Billy stopped and thought for a minute. Then he started again. "Slavery was an industry. Why do you think white people wanted, no, needed slaves? It was an industry. Slaves helped them make money. It's always about money. The white man owned slaves for the sole purpose of making and saving money." Uncle Billy paused again. He knew his little nephew never heard someone talk about slavery like this before. He did not want to rush this lesson.

"The slave owners didn't feed the slaves slave food. They didn't say, 'Oh, we got to the grocery store and pick up some slave food' like you do when you run out of dog food. You know, 'Did you remember to pick up the dog food?' Oh, noooo. What?! They fed the slaves to keep them alive—they had to work so they had to eat, but they didn't eat good food. The slaves ate whatever food was leftover or what the white man didn't eat. They threw them Negroes the pig entrails, what they call chittlins, the cow's brains, the chicken neck, chicken feet—all of that. Parts of the chicken no one with good sense would want to eat. And now look---Negroes still eating that stuff today."

"Hmmm. Well I don't." Ross said. "You don't what?" Asked Billy.

"I don't eat that stuff. I'm a vegetarian." Ross said with a smile.

"You a vegetarian?" Uncle Billy stared back towards the window in his family room.

"I am." A hesitant Ross answered.

57

"You are now. After I got on your mother about all that junk she was giving you when you were small." Uncle Billy reminded Ross.

"So I have a question." Ross was enjoying this history lesson and wanted to lighten the mood. "What the big deal with the 'N-word.'"

"The what!?" Uncle Billy had no idea what his nephew was talking about. "You know. The N-word." Ross opened his hands as if to say, 'you know.'

"Boy, what are you talking about?" A seemingly frustrated Uncle Billy asked.

"Uncle B! You going to make me say it?"

"Say what, Boy?" Uncle B acted as though he had no idea what Ross was talking about.

"Nigga! Uncle B. Nigga. Nigga, nigga, nigga, nigga, nigga. What's the big deal with that word?" Ross felt embarrassed at first saying it. It was like he was cursing, but the more he said it the better he felt saying it. He tried to hold back his smile.

Uncle B just stared at Ross with a deadpan look on his face, shaking his head. He signed, "Oh, Lord."

"What, Uncle B? I hear people say it all the time—well, not people. I hear black people say it and I know no other race is supposed to say it, but I don't know why. Auntie January told me that no one is supposed to say that word, but every black person I know says it. I'm confused." Ross was being sincere.

"Why you think, Boy?" Uncle Billy asked Ross. "I really don't know. I mean, it's just a word."

"It's not a word, Boy. It's a name. It's a name that they called slaves." Uncle Billy said in a soft tone.

"Ummmm…didn't they call slaves 'boy' too? No one says anything about that." Ross reasoned.

"Because you still have boys today. You a boy. They called grown men boys, which is not acceptable today. You won't hear a white man calling a black man a boy. That's just as bad if not worse than calling him a nigga." Uncle Billy explained.

"Ooooh! You said the N-word!" Ross quipped. Uncle Billy just shook his head.

"I'd rather be called the N-word than the other acceptable N-word." Ross said to his Uncle.

"What are you talking about now, Boy?" Uncle Billy was puzzled. "I'd rather be called N-word than the other N-word?" Ross repeated himself.

"What's the other N-word?" Uncle Billy was really confused now. "Negro. That word just sounds like a slave." Ross said.

Uncle Billy rolled his eyes.

"It does! It is not a cool sounding word—or name. When I hear the word 'negro' I think of really dark-skinned, big red-lipped, nappy afro having slaves. I'm sorry. I just do." Ross explained.

"I don't know---I don't know what to say to you right now. I think I am about to call your mother to come get you." Uncle Billy had it.

"Uncle B! I'm being serious right now. People get all up in arms about the N-word but they are like totally okay with saying Negro. You remember that poem you made me read one year---the Negro Speaks of Rivers? There's something about that word "negro" that reminds me of slaves. When you were talking about the Negro Spiritual earlier all I could do is think about slaves.

Sorry.

Uncle Billy was still in shock by what just came out of his young nephew's mouth. Maybe it was the generation.

"Listen here. White people used the word nigger as a derogatory name for slaves. The correct word or name or term for slaves, the acceptable name, was 'negro' but the unacceptable name was nigger. That is why black people get so offended now when a white person refers to a black person by that name." Uncle Billy explained.

"But white people don't refer to black people by that name." Ross did not understand.

"Not now. It's a hate name. If a white person uses that word they are, more than likely, being hateful." Uncle Billy said.

"And what about when a black person uses it? Black people use it all the time. Like all the time. And sometimes they're using it when they are mad at another black person." Ross asked.

"It's not a racial hate. It's a loving hate." Uncle Billy looked away realizing that what he just said did not sound like it made sense.

Ross gave Uncle Billy a look. "A loving hate, huh? Yeah, it makes no sense to me."

"Black people in this country have their own demons they deal with. Families fight. Families fuss. But being a slave is a totally different kind of demon. No black person wants any verbal relics of slavery. Hearing a white person call a black person a nigga or worse, a nigger is too painful and offensive. Negro might remind you of a slave, but nigger coming out of the mouth of a non-black reminds me of slavery. You might be too young to understand that, Son." Billy sat back.

"I think I get it. But I wonder what would happen if black people did not hold on to that memory. Like, what if white people did say it and it didn't bother anyone? Then what?" Ross was reasoning out loud. He was a thinker, quite the thinker for being only 13 years old.

"I don't know, Ross. I don't know." Uncle Billy stood up. "Your mother just pulled up to the driveway. Tell me that name I gave you." Uncle Billy asked Ross.

"Let me think---oh, Carter Woodson?" Ross said in a question.

"You got it. Come give me a hug, Boy." Uncle Billy put his big hand on

Ross's head and the two embraced. "And yes, you can bring your X-Box to the house on Monday. Bring something I can play too. You can teach me something for once. I'm tired of always schooling you."

Ross hugged his Uncle and thanked him. "Oh, I have a lot of games I can teach you to play. You'll like it. But your hands might be too big for the controller. We'll see. Thanks for the lesson on black history. See you on Monday!" Ross picked up his book bag and was headed out the door when he stopped and said, "See you later my favorite N-word!" He laughed and darted out to his mother's car.

Chapter 6

The Most Important Word in Any Language: Lesson on Attitude

"Ross! Come on in here, Ross!"

Uncle Billy was sitting in his old blue recliner in his living room, and Ross was in the kitchen eating his afternoon snack and reading one of the magazines his uncle usually made him read while he waited for his mother to pick him up after school. Uncle Billy was calling Ross into the room where he was to ask him a question. Ross put another handful of his cashews into his mouth before he walked into the living room where is uncle was seated.

"What's up, Uncle B?" Ross said while chewing on his cashews. "What you got going on this weekend?" Uncle Billy asked Ross.

"Let's see. I'm pretty sure I have homework, chores, church, and more homework. You know. The usual." Ross made his way to the sofa, dropped himself down and threw up his right leg to get comfortable.

"Sounds like a busy weekend," Uncle Billy said, clearly unimpressed. 'Well, what can I say? I'm a busy kid." Ross smiled.

"Well, Busy Kid. Do you think you can find the time to come help me cut the grass this weekend?" Uncle Billy asked his nephew.

"Seriously, Uncle B? What happened to the guy who you usually get to cut it?"

Ross hated cutting grass. School was almost out for the summer so it was already getting hot, and Uncle Billy had a push lawn mower with a very large yard. Why he wouldn't buy a driving lawnmower was anyone's guess. Maybe he did not buy a driving lawnmower because he did not have anywhere to house it. Either way, when it came time to cut the grass, he used a push lawnmower to cut his near acre-sized yard. Ross once helped his uncle cut the grass with the push lawn mower and hated every minute of it.

"He's sick. He's been sick for a few weeks now. I can't wait for him. It's not his grass. It's my grass and it looks bad. And since you're over here more than he is, I think it only makes sense for your narrow behind to help cut it.

What you say? You goin' ta help your uncle out?" Uncle Billy asked.

Ross rolled his entire head and then threw himself backwards on the couch to layout flat. "I guesssssssssss-ah." Ross stressed the word to where it sounded like it was a much longer word than it really is.

"Ross! Boy, what's wrong with you?" Uncle Billy was taken aback by Ross's histrionic outburst.

"Nothing!" Ross stressed the 'ing' to clearly sound disgusted by the idea of having to cut grass this weekend. "You know I hate cutting grass!" Ross was still lying on his back on the couch with his forearm bent over his eyes so Uncle Billy could not see his face.

"Let me ask you something, Boy." Uncle Billy sat up in his recliner. "Do you know what's the most important word in the world?" (This came out of nowhere.) Uncle Billy would sometimes ask Ross questions that seemed to come out of the blue. This was one of those times.

Without moving a peep and with his forearm still over his eyes, Ross just groaned. "Uuuuugggggghhh!"

"Wrong! Try again!" Uncle Billy snapped. Ross still didn't move or answer.

"I'm talking to you, Boy! Answer me, hear?" Uncle Billy was now getting frustrated.

"I don't know!" Ross retorted, still lying on his back with his forearm over his eyes.

"Then take a wild guess, Ross!" shouted Uncle Billy. "Money!" Ross said still on his back with his eyes covered. "What did you say, Boy?" Uncle Billy asked Ross.

Ross, not moving and still with his eyes covered by his forearm, did not answer his uncle.

"I said, what did you say, Boy?" Uncle Billy shouted.

"Money!" Ross finally sat up, but was slouched in the sofa, but at least he was now looking at his uncle.

"You trying to tell me you want money to cut the grass? Is that what you saying to me, Ross?" Uncle Billy was offended.

"No!" Ross really wasn't saying that. "You asked me a question. I am answering your question," Ross said, trying not to raise his voice or sound disrespectful.

"Well, the answer to your answer is 'no.' You're wrong. Guess again." Uncle Billy was not as offended, realizing Ross was not asking for money.

"You know, I don't know, Uncle B. I don't know." Ross was ready to go home by now.

"The most important word is—where's your phone, Boy?"

Ross rolled his eyes, then put his hand in his pocket and took out his phone. He knew the routine.

"Write this down. The most important word in the human language, and that means in every language on the planet earth—the most important word is— attitude. Write that down! A-t-t-i-t-u-d-e. Attitude, Dude. Write!" Uncle sat back and looked at his nephew with a proud look on his face for the rhyming words he just used.

Ross rolled his eyes.

"And write this down too. Write down this name." Uncle Billy just remembered something else so he sat up. "Write down William James. You ever heard of William James, Boy?" Uncle Billy asked.

"No." Ross was not very happy right now.

"I know you haven't. Write down his name. You gonna learn today." Uncle Billy demanded of Ross. "William James. Two first names. William and James." Uncle Billy waited to see Ross typing in his phone. Then he continued. "William James is one of the greatest psychiatrists or psychologists—I can't remember--to ever live. They used to call him 'the father of psychology.' They still call him that. Write that name down."

Uncle Billy paused for a minute then started again. "William James said this about attitude—he said, 'The greatest discovery of my generation is that human beings can alter their lives by altering their attitudes of mind.' What!?!!?!" Uncle Billy got excited. "Did you hear that, Boy? A man or woman, boy or girl, can change their entire lives by changing their attitude! That right there is nothing but the truth." Uncle Billy sat back as he reflected on what he just told Ross. "And I can tell you right now, you need to change your attitude."

Ross was staring at his uncle's excitement with something of a look of puzzlement on his face. He did not know what to think about what he just heard, and he definitely did not know what to say to that.

"I didn't see you write that in your phone. Did you get all of that, Boy?" Uncle Billy asked Ross.

"Uh…" Ross blinked a few times as if to come back to wherever he was in his thoughts and said, "I got his name down. I did not get the rest. What was it again?"

Uncle Billy just shook his head. "'The greatest discovery!' Type it!" Uncle Billy shouted. "'Of my generation.'" Uncle Billy paused to wait for Ross to stop typing. "'Is.'" Uncle Billy stopped again.

"Okay. Go ahead." Ross was ready for him to finish.

"'That human beings can alter their lives by altering their attitudes of mind.' You need me to say that again, Ross?" Uncle Billy asked.

Ross kept typing the statement in his phone under his many notes that his uncle would make him keep. "No. I got it," Ross said as he put down his phone.

"Or you can just write this—you can alter your life by altering your attitude—then put William James after that. All you need to know is that you can change your entire life by changing your attitude. So write that down." Uncle Billy sat back after he gave his instructions.

Ross had already typed the full sentence so he did not bother typing the rephrased portion his uncle just said.

"I don't see you typing!" Uncle Billy shouted. "I typed it already!" Ross whined.

"You didn't type what I just said, Boy. Type this, too! You can alter your life by altering your attitude. Because Lord knows you need to alter your attitude."

Ross picked back up his phone and typed, "You can alter your life by altering your attitude."

"If you have a good, positive attitude," Uncle Billy continued, "you will have a good, positive life. If you have a nasty attitude, you will have a nasty life. It's just that simple. And if you want a better life—guess what? Then have a better attitude. It's that simple," Uncle Billy said as he sat back into his recliner. But he wasn't finished.

"Everything about you—and this is a fact." Uncle Billy was looking at his young nephew but his young nephew wasn't looking at him. Ross was tired and ready to go home. He still wasn't happy about having to cut his uncle's grass.

But Uncle Billy continued.

"Everything about you—your house, your neighborhood, your clothes, your car, your friends, your job—everything in your life is an exact mirror of your attitude. If you have nasty, rude friends, it's because you have a nasty attitude. If you have a nasty teacher teaching your class, guess what? It's because you have a nasty attitude in class."

"Are you saying I have a nasty attitude?" Ross asked, pretending to be into what his uncle was teaching.

"Do you have a nasty teacher? If you do, then that's exactly what I'm saying," Uncle Ross retorted. "Your life is a reflection, a perfect reflection of your attitude. Let me tell you a story."

"A guy named Ed was headed out of town one day when his car started to over heat. He pulled his car to the side of the road and decided he would wait it out—you know—turn the car off and let it cool down a bit.

"As he sat in his car waiting for it to cool, a car headed in the direction to go into his town pulls up to Ed's car and stops. A man stepped out of the car, and seeing Ed sitting on the hood of his car asked, 'Need any help?'

"Ed said, 'No, I'm good. Just waiting for my car to cool down. I'll be headed back on the road in a li'l bit. But thanks for asking.'

"The stranger then asked Ed, 'You from round here?' "Ed said, 'Yep. Lived here my whole life.'

"The stranger explained to Ed that it was his first time visiting this town and asked, 'what kind of folks you got living around here?'

"Ed asked the man, 'Well, stranger, what kind of folks was there in the town you came from?'

"The stranger said, 'well, there was mostly a low-down, lying, thieving, gossiping, backbiting lot of people in my town, let me tell you.'

"After a few seconds Ed said, 'Well, stranger, that's about the kind of folks you'll find in this town.'

"After hearing that, the stranger got in his car and drove back in the direction where he came."

Uncle Billy paused for a brief moment and then started the story back up. "A few minutes later another car comes down the road. The driver sees

Ed sitting in his car and stops to offer help. 'Need any help?'

"'Oh, no. I'm just sitting here waiting for my car to cool down. Making sure my radiator don't over heat. I'll be on my way out of town in a li'l while here.'

"'Okay. I'm headed into town. You live in this town?' the stranger asked Ed.

"'Oh, yes. Lived here all my life.'

"'Well, tell me, what kind of folks you got living around here?'

"'Well, stranger, what kind of folks was there in the town you come from?' Ed asked.

"The stranger said, "well, there was a mostly decent, hardworking, law-abiding, friendly lot of people in the town I came from.'

"Ed said, 'well, stranger, that's about the kind of folk you'll find around here in this town.'

"The stranger thanks the guy, gets in his car, and drives into town."

Uncle Billy stopped and allowed that story to sink into Ross' mind. What just happened in that story, Boy?

Ross sat thinking for a minute. "I get it," Ross said calmly.

"You get what? What happened?" Uncle Billy asked Ross again.

"Each stranger. Each guy who—wait a minute. So the first guy saw low- down, dirty people in his town, and so Ed told him that those were the kind of people that he will find in this town. The second guy said that in his town he saw good, honest people, and so Ed said that's what you will find in this town." Ross recited the story.

"That's the story, but what happened, Ross?" Uncle Billy shouted. "That's what happened!" Ross sort of shouted back.

"But why, Boy? It's the same town! Why did Ed tell one man that he would find decent, friendly people in the same town that he told the other guy he would find low-down, lying, thieving rascals?" Uncle Billy sounded frustrated like he usually does when Ross does not seem to catch on to his stories.

Ross sat for a minute thinking. "I guess…I guess whatever each guy saw….no, wait. The first guy thought most people in his town were low-down, lying somebodies and so he figured most everyone was a low-down, lying somebody?"

"That's right, Boy. The first man had a negative attitude towards people so the people he met would either be negative or else he would paint them as negative. The second man had a positive attitude towards people so the people he met was either positive or else he would see them in a positive light. It's all about attitude." Uncle Billy sat back to allow all of what he just taught Ross to sink in.

"A great attitude is what you need to be successful, Son. That's what you need. Any successful person you know had a positive attitude before success.

You don't become successful and then have a great attitude. You become successful because of a great attitude. So what does that mean? It means when I asked you to cut the grass you should have jumped up and been happy about it! Had a great attitude about cutting grass. Why? Because great things would follow."

"Happy about cutting the grass? Seriously, Uncle B?" Ross asked, still not in any form or fashion excited about cutting grass in the heat.

"Yes! That's the key, Boy! That is the secret to success. We've talked about this before. You want to do great things, for yourself, for your mother—you talk about that all the time, Son. If you want to do something great, you first have to be great. And the way you become great is by having a great attitude.

Your attitude is what you are right now. Have you ever seen someone with a bad attitude? I know you have," Uncle Billy asked Ross.

"Oh, yeah! Don't ask me who though." Ross gave his uncle the side-eyed look.

"I already know. Your mother sometimes has a bad attitude. But do you

know why your mother has a bad attitude?" Uncle Billy asked Ross. Ross' mother could be—hot-tempered and short with Ross at times.

"I have no idea," Ross said.

"Because your mother never learned what I am trying to teach you right now. Your mother is reactive instead of proactive. I'm trying to teach you to be proactive. If you get a bad grade on a quiz or test, don't get mad and upset. Flip it around and be happy. Be happy that you now know what you did wrong so when the final test comes you'll know the answers. Look for the positive in everything and watch happens. I promise you, you will see all sorts of good things come your way. Your positive attitude will be the cause of positive results. It has to. It's a law, like the law of gravity. If you jump off the house 100 times, 100 times you will fall to the ground. Not one time will you float up. It's a law. It has to happen. If you have a positive attitude, positive results will follow. It has to." Uncle Billy liked to refer to the law of gravity. He believed in laws.

"Hmmm. You know what, Uncle B?" asked Ross. "What's that, Boy?"

"I am so excited about Monday! I get to cut your grass!" Ross said in a surprisingly excited voice.

Uncle Billy stared at his young nephew trying to figure out if he was being sarcastic or serious.

"In fact, I'm going to ask Ma if she will bring me over on Sunday so I can start on Sunday and finish it on Monday." Ross jumped up from the sofa to walk over to the front door to look out at the yard. "Yeah, I'll start on that side on Sunday." Ross was looking to the right of the yard. "Then I'll finish up this side and the back on Monday." Ross turned around to look at his puzzled uncle.

Uncle Billy did not know what to make of what Ross was saying. "Well, yeah—yeah, you can do that," a flustered and bewildered Uncle Billy said.

Ross just smiled at his uncle.

"And when you get done, I—I have a little something for you," Uncle Billy said hesitatingly not knowing for sure what to make of Ross' sudden change in behavior. He wasn't sure if it was genuine or not, but he was pleased.

Did Ross get it that quickly? Did he understand? Would he now forever be positive with everything? Uncle Billy doubted that. But even if Ross was faking it, it was a start. Uncle Billy knew that even with Ross just playing around, if that was what Ross was doing, just by practicing being positive, Ross would be lead to bigger and better things in life. He would reward Ross for keeping this great, positive attitude. He would give him more money than he has ever given him—not to play along with the game, but because he was so darn happy with his young nephew.

As he sat there pondering these thoughts in his mind, Ross' mother pulled up the driveway.

"Well, here comes Ma." Ross ran into the kitchen to grab his book bag. "I'll see you on Sunday, Uncle B!" Ross ran out the front door. Uncle Billy stood up and watched his young nephew run to his mother's car, still astounded at how quickly the power of attitude had worked with Ross. He just shook his head and smiled, relearning this old lesson himself.

Chapter 7

Broke versus Poor: Lesson on Money

"Uncle B!" Ross came running into the front door of his uncle's house after school. "Uncle B! Uncle B!"

Ross was excited and desperately needed to ask his uncle for what he believed to be a huge favor.

"Uncle B!"

Ross ran into the kitchen. Sometimes Ross would find his uncle at the kitchen table or washing dishes at the sink, but today, Uncle Billy was not in the kitchen either.

"Uncle B!?" Ross yelled out and then paused to see if he would hear his uncle respond back or at least hear him walking around in the house. Nothing. "Uncle B?"

A few minutes of silence and Ross heard a toilet flush from the bathroom in the back of the house.

"Is that you yelling out my name like I owe you money?" An agitated Uncle Billy said, as he came walking out of the bathroom, drying his hands with a paper towel. "I heard you the first time. Can a man use the bathroom in peace? You yelling out my name like I'm supposed to answer to you."

Uncle Billy walked by his young nephew, out of the kitchen, and into the living room and was headed to his recliner. Uncle Billy plopped himself down in his recliner, reclined the chair back, and turned to look at Ross. "Now. What got you hollering my name out like you my daddy?"

Ross darted to the sofa next to his uncle's recliner and full of excitement said, "Uncle B, guess what?"

"Mm-Hmm. I'm listening." Uncle B was just as calm as Ross was excited. "So, remember how I've been wanting to visit Washington, D.C. for the last—forever?" Ross's eyes were the size of silver dollars as he leaned towards his uncle waiting for his uncle to give an answer so he can finish with his story.

"Mm-Hmm," Uncle Billy acknowledged. "Well guess what?" Ross quickly asked.

Uncle Billy didn't say a word because he knew what Ross was going to tell him anyway. So he just looked at his nephew.

"Well, our school is taking a field trip to D.C.!" Ross was elated and could not hold back his excitement. Upon saying the news, Ross jumped up from the sofa and did a happy dance right there in front of his uncle.

"Oh, well, that's great, Son. You get to go to the nation's capital. When you all going?" Uncle Billy asked Ross.

"Well…" Ross sat back down on the sofa next to his uncle's recliner. "Our 8th grade class is going during the week of our spring break, so this coming March," Ross explained to his uncle.

"Well isn't that nice," Uncle Billy said with a smile. "You'll have a great time. You know, I lived there for a short time? Yeah, back in the '70s. Be sure you go to all the museums. I know that's why they probably taking you all up there. Pay attention and take notes on that phone of yours." Uncle Billy pulled his glasses out of his shirt pocket, put his glasses on his face, and reached for his magazine that was sitting on the nearby coffee table.

"I will, Uncle B." Ross sat silent for a moment, looking down and then said, "Hey Uncle, B!"

His uncle, turning through the pages of his ESPN magazine, responded with, "What's that?" without turning to look at Ross.

"Do you—do you think I can borrow $700?" Ross' head dropped as he asked his uncle for the money.

Uncle Ross dropped his magazine down to his lap and looked at Ross from over his glasses. "What you say, Boy?"

"Nothing, Uncle B." Ross sat back and looked out the door as if he heard something outside, but he didn't hear anything outside. He was just embarrassed to ask for money and hated asking his uncle for so much money.

Seven hundred dollars seemed like a fortune to Ross.

Uncle Billy picked back up his magazine and started reading again.

It was quiet for about a good minute when Ross said out loud, "I hate being poor!"

Uncle Billy put his magazine down again on his lap and looked at Ross over the top of his glasses. "You said you hate what, Boy?" Uncle Billy asked.

"I hate being poor!" Ross said again sounding somewhat frustrated. "Who said you was poor?" Uncle Billy asked Ross looking at him from over the top rim of his glasses.

"What do you mean? We are poor, Uncle B," Ross said. "Who's poor?" Uncle Billy asked again.

"We're poor!" Ross said.

"We?" Uncle Billy asked. "As in you and me?"

"Well, no. Not you. I am. Me and mom are poor," Ross said sounding pitiful.

"Why you think you and your mother are poor?" Uncle Billy asked Ross. "Because. We don't have enough money," Ross answered.

"Enough money for what?" Uncle Billy asked Ross sounding frustrated and confused and still carrying on the conversation looking at Ross from over his reading glasses.

"Well, just for things," Ross said, looking down at his feet.

"Things like what, Boy?" Uncle Billy asked. "Don't you have everything you need? Did somebody call you poor?"

"Well, like this trip. I know mom doesn't have $700 so I don't even know if I am going to be able to go." Ross dropped his head again.

Uncle Billy picked his magazine back up and started reading again. Ross looked at his uncle and rolled his entire head, not his eyes, but his entire head. He hated when his uncle would ignore him like this. He just let his uncle know that he needed the money to go on this dream trip of his, but his uncle did not say a word.

"Well?" Ross asked his uncle.

"Well what?" Uncle Billy responded, still reading his magazine. "Nothing!" a frustrated Ross pouted out. Ross stood up from the sofa and walked into kitchen. Uncle Billy didn't move an inch. He was into his magazine. Ross later walked back into the living room where his uncle sat and asked, "Uncle B, can I borrow $700 so I can go on this trip?"

Without looking up from his magazine, Uncle Billy responded quick and calm with, "No."

Ross paused for a few seconds. "Are you being serious right now?" Ross sounded surprised.

"I am," Uncle Billy answered, again without bothering to look up from his magazine.

"Why not?" asked Ross, sounding upset.

"Because," Uncle Billy said again quickly and calmly and without looking up from his magazine.

Ross was ready to snatch the magazine from his uncle's hands, but he knew better than to do that. But he was extremely frustrated at this point.

"Because what, Uncle B? You know I've been wanting to go to D.C. for all of my life." Ross was sounding desperate.

"Because…," Uncle Billy paused and then said, "Because I'm broke." Uncle Billy said while turning a page of his magazine.

"You're what?" Ross sounded even more frustrated.

"I am broke." Uncle Billy laid his magazine down on his lap and turned to Ross. "B-R-O-K-E. Broke. You know what broke is don't you, Boy?" Uncle Billy picked his magazine back up and started reading it.

Ross was bewildered and did not know what to say to his uncle. "Uncle Billy…" Ross sat staring at his uncle in disbelief. "So you're seriously going to not allow me to go to D.C.?"

"I'm not stopping you from going. You can go. Go on. Have fun." Uncle Billy turned to the next page.

"Uncle B! I can't go without money." Ross was angry and desperate.

How can his uncle be so calm about him not going to his dream trip? Ross was beside himself.

"So what does that have to do with me?" Uncle Billy asked sounding surprised.

"Nothing," snapped Ross, "Nothing at all." Ross sat back in the sofa and looked out the door again, while biting down on his teeth. Ross was so angry he could cry.

Uncle Billy, without looking at his nephew, turned the page of his magazine and said to his young nephew, "You didn't answer my question."

Ross turned to look at his uncle. He just stared at him not sure what he was talking about. "Are you talking to me?" Ross asked.

"Ah ha," Uncle Billy said. "What question?" asked Ross.

"I asked you, you do know what broke is don't you, Boy?"

Ross, looked at his uncle sideways and then turned his eyes back towards the door to look outside and said, "Yeah."

"Well, what does it mean?" Uncle Billy asked without looking at his nephew as he turned the page of his magazine.

Ross turned and looked at his uncle with a look of disgust and said, "It means you don't want me to go to D.C."

"Mm-hmm," Uncle Billy mumbled as he turned another page of his magazine, still not looking at his young nephew. Ross just sat on the sofa with a scour on his face staring out the front door. Just angry.

There was about 20 seconds of silence when Uncle Billy asked, "What else it mean?"

Ross turned to look at his uncle. "Broke means poor, Uncle Billy. I get it. I'm sorry. I didn't know you were poor, too. I shouldn't have asked you," Ross said in a frustrated, yet sarcastic tone.

Uncle Billy laid his magazine down and looked at Ross from over the rim of his glasses. "Who's poor? I ain't poor. You said your momma is poor. You said you were poor. But I'm not poor." Uncle Billy picked back up his magazine and started reading again.

"That's that you said!" Ross elevated his voice at his uncle.

"I said no such thing! I said I am broke. Broke. I even spelled it for your simple self. B-R-O-K-E. Broke." Uncle Billy shook his head and turned the page to his magazine.

"Really Uncle B?" asked Ross. "What's the difference between being broke and poor?"

"Well there you go," Uncle Billy said, as he laid his magazine back down. "That's what you need to be asking. 'What's the difference between being broke and being poor?' That's what you need to ask me." Uncle Billy picked back up his magazine.

"Well! I'm asking you—what's the difference?" Ross asked, sounding frustrated still.

"Well, I'll tell you like this right here," Uncle Billy said, while still looking at his magazine as if he was reading it. "Poor—it's a state of mind. It's a state of being. If you're poor, you don't have a thing." Uncle Billy turned a page, still not looking at his nephew. He continued.

"Poor people believe they have nothing. And to have nothing is to be nothing. Poor people got it bad. I'm not poor. I'm broke. Being broke is temporary. It's just what you are right at that moment. It's not a state of mind. You can have a million dollars up under your mattress, but if you're out with your friends and you didn't take any of your money with you, and somebody ask you for a dollar, 'Nah, Man. I'm broke'" Uncle Billy paused for a minute then said, "I'm not poor, but right now, I'm broke."

Ross sat quiet for a minute trying to understand what his uncle was telling him.

"So if I ask you for $700 tomorrow…." Ross stopped and looked at his uncle.

"Listen to me Ross." Uncle Billy laid his magazine down on his lap and looked at Ross over the top of his glasses. "You said you were poor, right? Did I hear you say that?"

"Yeah, I said that. I am. My mom is so I am," Ross said feeling a little embarrassed in saying it.

"Okay. Let me help you out." Uncle Billy sat up in his recliner. "You know the routine." Uncle Billy stopped and waited for Ross.

Ross just looked at his uncle and then remembered—he wanted him to take out his phone and take notes. Ross reached into his pocket and took out his iPhone. He was not about to act up right now because he had a sense that his uncle was going to give him the money he needed after this lecture.

"Okay, I'm ready," Ross politely said.

"The very first thing you need to get into your thick head, Son, is you are not poor! Stop saying that. I don't ever want to hear you say those words again. I don't care if all you got is one pair of draws and a t-shirt—you are not poor.

You might be broke. You might not have money right now, but you are rich! Put that thought in your mind. You hear me?" Uncle Billy stopped to get a response from his nephew.

Ross was typing what his uncle was telling him in his phone and then stopped to answer his uncle. "Yeah, I hear you. But…" Ross paused.

"But what?! There are no buts. You are not poor. Type that in your phone. 'I am not poor!' Type that." Uncle Billy waited and watched as Ross typed.

"Now. Do you believe that, Ross?" Uncle Billy asked Ross.

"Honestly? Not at all. Mom says we are all the time. It's why she cuts my hair and I cannot get a professional haircut," Ross said.

"Well, let your momma be poor then. Just because your momma believes she's poor, does not mean you have to believe it. The first thing you have to do is believe that you are not poor. In fact, believe that you are rich. Believe you have all the money you want and need. That's the first step for not being poor— believing you're not poor. And the way you believe you are not poor is to start thinking that you're not poor. Start thinking rich, Boy." Uncle Billy stopped to allow what he was telling Ross to sink in— and for him to type it in his phone.

"The way you start believing something is to start thinking something.

80

Write this down—a belief ain't nothing but an accepted thought. If you repeat a thought over and over and over again, guess what? You begin to believe it.

Your mother been telling you that you all are poor for so long you believe it. I'm telling you you're rich. Start telling yourself you're rich. Tell yourself every day all day that you are rich. Tell yourself you got all the money. When you hear your mother say you all are poor, tell yourself, "I'm not poor. I'm rich.' Every day, Ross. You hearing me?"

Ross nodded his head.

"Did you write that in your phone? Write, 'tell myself I am rich every day, all day.'" Uncle Billy stopped to allow Ross to type that message in his phone. "I don't care. No matter what, you have to start saying that. Let me ask you something. Do you know French?" Uncle Billy sat back in his recliner and waited for Ross to answer.

"Huh?" Ross asked puzzled.

"Do you know how to speak French? Wee or no?" Uncle Billy asked.

Ross rolled his eyes. "No, Uncle B. Come on." Ross knew enough to know that 'wee' meant yes in French.

"What do you think will happen if you moved to France or Haiti—you do know they speak French in Haiti, don't you, Boy?" Uncle Billy asked Ross. Ross just shrugged his shoulders. "What do you think will happen if you lived in one of these French-speaking countries and heard nothing but French all day, every day?"

"Uh, I'll start speaking French," Ross said unenthusiastically.

"That's right! So start hearing yourself speak rich so you can start living rich. Every day, all day. That's the first step. Once you start saying it, you'll start believing it—in time." Uncle Billy sat back and folded his arms on his lap.

"Got it. What's next?" Ross said, waiting for the end of this lecture so he can know whether his uncle was going to give him the money for his trip.

"I don't even know if I want to go on to the next step with you, Ross," Uncle Billy said.

"Why not?" a surprised Ross said.

"Because I want you to focus on this one step. You really have to start changing the way you think, Boy. Walking around here talking about 'I'm poor.' You sound pathetic. Don't ever say that again, you hear me?" Uncle Billy was really disgusted with Ross for that. "Don't you ever say that again!" Uncle Billy had to say it one more time.

"I got it, Uncle B. What's the next thing you want me to type in my phone?" Ross asked politely.

"You already started the next step—I hope." Uncle Billy stopped. "Um…I'm not sure what you mean," Ross said.

"Saving! Save your money. Saving is the antidote for being poor. Saving is the vaccination for poverty. As long as you save, guess what? You have money. So save. And the money you been saving, tell your mother to open you up a bank account where you can put your money," Uncle Billy told his nephew.

"She did already! I have a bank account, Uncle Billy," Ross said proudly. "You do? When did you do that?" Uncle Billy asked.

"About a month ago. I put all the money I have saved in my account. I have $68 in my account. And it's great. You can cashapp me the money for my trip right through your "—Ross paused for a second—"phone. Do you have cashapp, Uncle B?"

"I never heard of a cashapp," Uncle Billy said looking confused.

"It's really great. I'll tell you more about it after you finish. So I have to tell myself every day I am rich and I have to save. What's next?" Ross was

82

enjoying this simply because he believed he was going to get the money for his trip for listening intently to his uncle.

Uncle B sat back and looked out the window to his left as if he was thinking of what to tell his young nephew. He knew this lesson was an important lesson. He paused for a moment then he said, without even looking at Ross, "Start dreaming."

There was a silence for about five seconds and then Ross said, "Okay.

Dreaming about what?" Ross asked.

"Just start dreaming, Son. Dream about where you want to live. Dream about what you want to do in life. Dream about what you want to be. Just dream. And get into your dream. See yourself going to D.C. See yourself with the things you want. See your mother with the things she wants. See yourself happy and doing what you want to do. Every day, just dream and when dreaming, get into the dream—live it until you feel it."

Uncle Billy, still staring out the window, was telling his young nephew this advice while apparently reminiscing about something—he was deep in thought and speaking at the same time.

"Okaaaay." Ross said. "I can definitely do that. I've been dreaming about going to D.C. quite a bit these past few months…I mean years. And I feel it too! All the museums, the monuments, the Lincoln Memorial." Ross knew a lot about the Nation's Capital. Ross looked at his uncle from the side of his eyes.

"Believe you'll be rich and you'll be rich, Son. Stop telling yourself you're poor. Dream and dream often. Stay focused on your dreams. Don't dream—" Uncle Billy paused and then started back up again. "Don't dream of going to

D.C. one week then change and start dreaming of going to L.A. the next week. Stick with the dream, the desire, that's it—stick with the desire, Ross. And don't stop dreaming just because of an obstacle. Don't stop dreaming and don't stop believing when someone tells you, 'no.' No is nothing but an obstacle. Failure is nothing but an obstacle. Keep going and believing."

Ross's stomach dropped. Was his uncle telling him no again?

"Did you know that Thomas Edison—" Uncle Billy paused. "You do know who Thomas Edison is, don't you boy?" Uncle Billy stopped to ask Ross this question. "Well? You know who Thomas Edison is?"

"Of course, I know who Thomas Edison is. Duh," Ross said. "Who?" Uncle Billy asked.

"Everybody knows Thomas Edison, Uncle B. Go ahead with the story," Ross said. It seemed as though Ross really did not know who Thomas Edison was, but just didn't want his uncle to know.

"Boy, if you don't tell me who—"

"Thomas Edison was an American inventor and businessman. One of the greatest inventors," Ross interrupted his uncle. Uncle Billy just stared at his nephew. "What did he invent?" Uncle Billy asked Ross, keeping a close eye on him.

"He—" Ross began to answer then he looked down at his phone again and said, "the light bulb. He invented the light bulb." Ross concluded and smiled.

"That's a dang shame." Uncle Billy sat back. "What?" Ross said acting surprised.

"You looked at your phone," Uncle Billy said with a look of disgust. "Who?" Ross asked sounding guilty. Uncle Billy just shook his head. "Thomas Edison tried ten thousand times, failed ten thousand times, but never gave up on his dream of a lamp that could operate by electricity. Once you have your dream, don't give up on it," Uncle Billy told his young nephew.

"Wow! Uncle B. I didn't know that. Yes, I am never giving up on my dream—of going to D.C.," Ross said and then sat quietly waiting for confirmation that his uncle was going to give him the money to go.

"That's right. Don't. You'll get to D.C. one year. Might not be this year. Might not be next year. But guess what? You'll get there. One day. I promise you that." Uncle Billy took his glasses out of his pocket and picked back up his magazine.

Ross could not believe that his ucle did not offer to pay his way to D.C. He felt a little sick to his stomach, but—he wasn't going to give up. He was going to go to D.C. and he was going with his class. He felt hopeful. There was still seven months before the trip. His thinking had already begun to change. He believed he would go and nothing was going to stop him. Nothing.